DELITEFUL COLORING

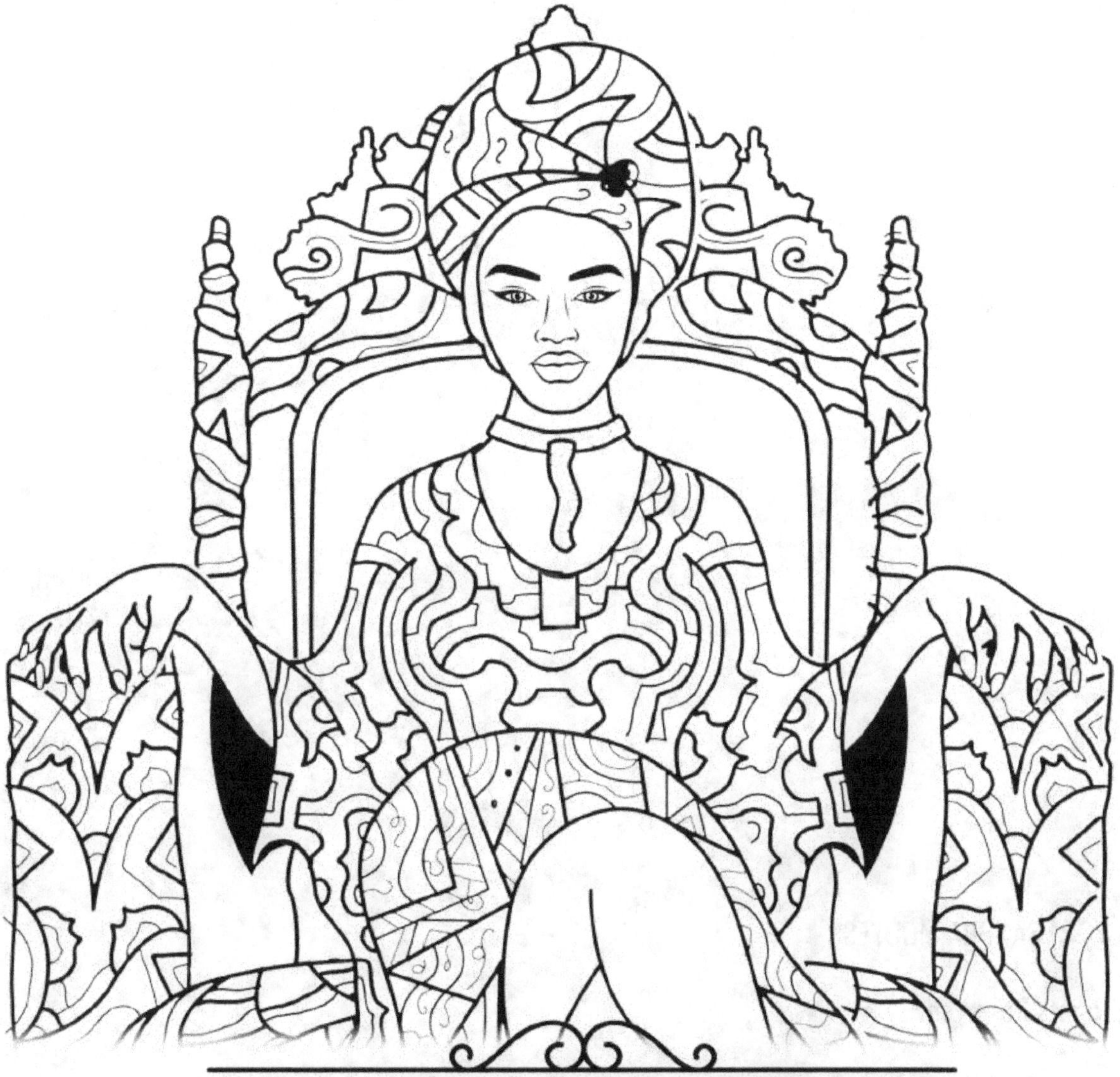

MELANIN MAGIC
A SELF CARE COLORING BOOK
FOR BLACK WOMEN

by Sandra Mcdyess

DELITEFUL COLORING - MELANIN MAGIC A SELF CARE COLORING BOOK FOR BLACK WOMEN

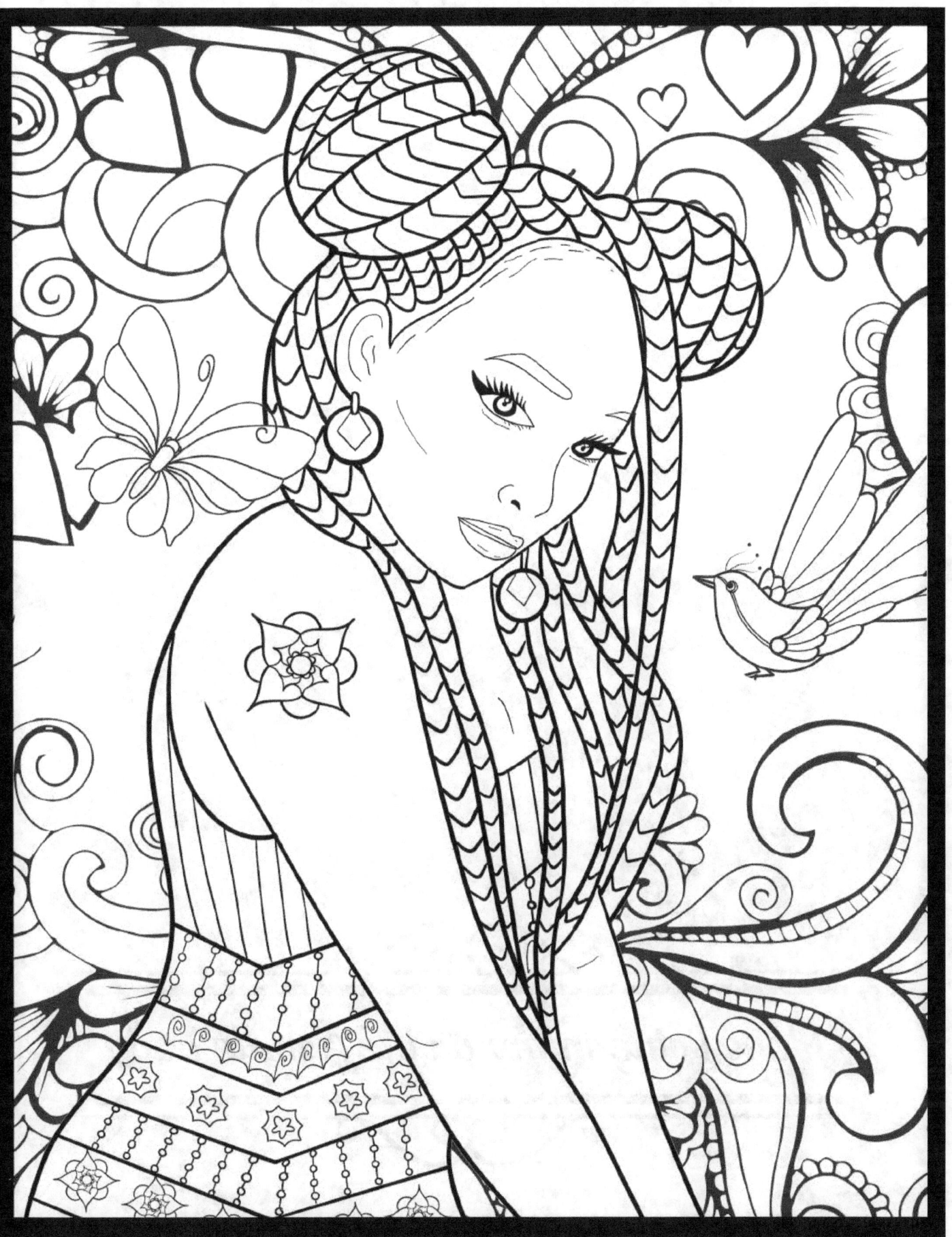

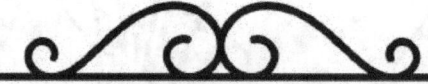

I love living in my divine female body

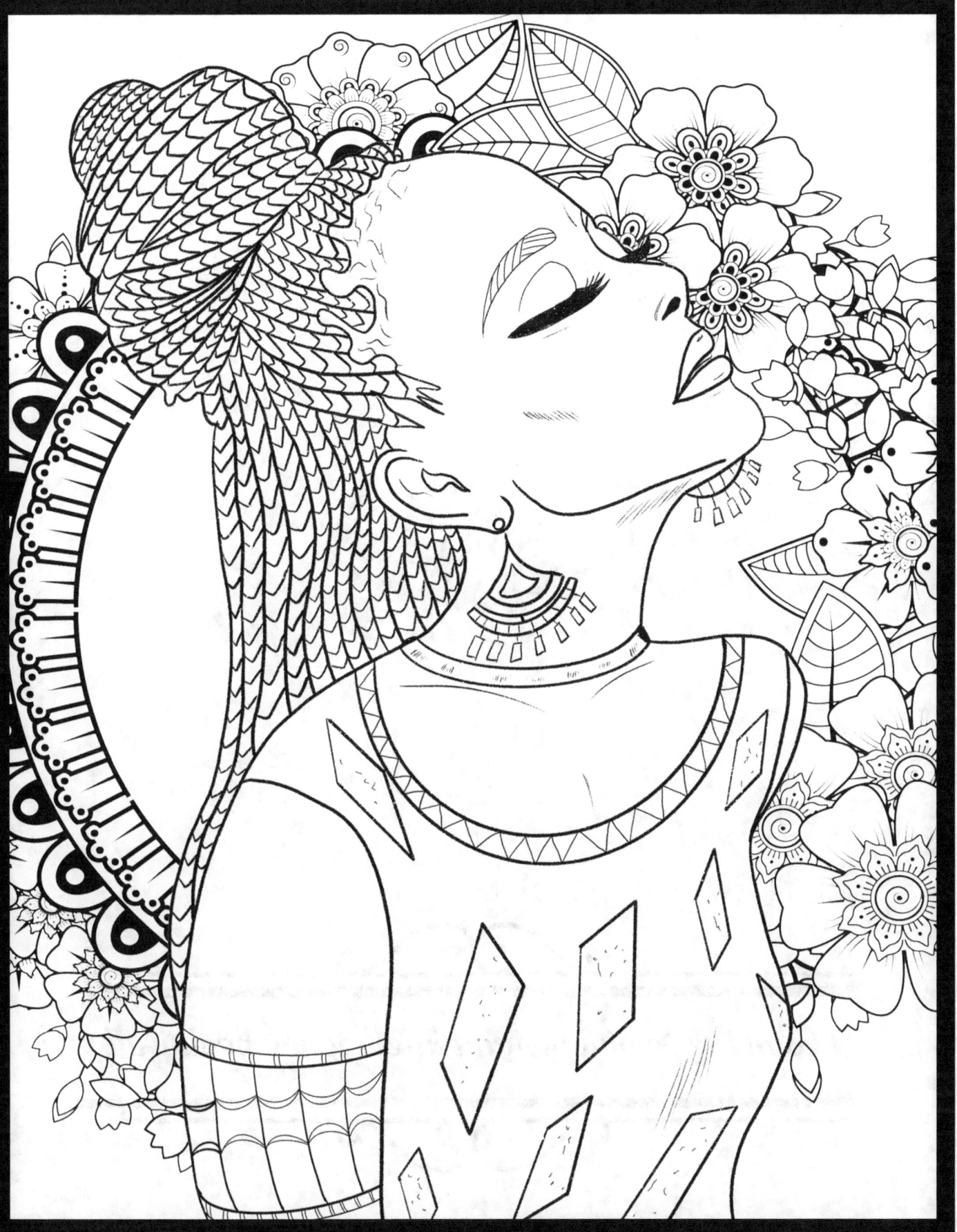

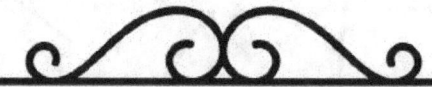

I combine femininity and intelligence beautifully

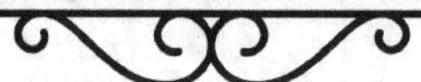

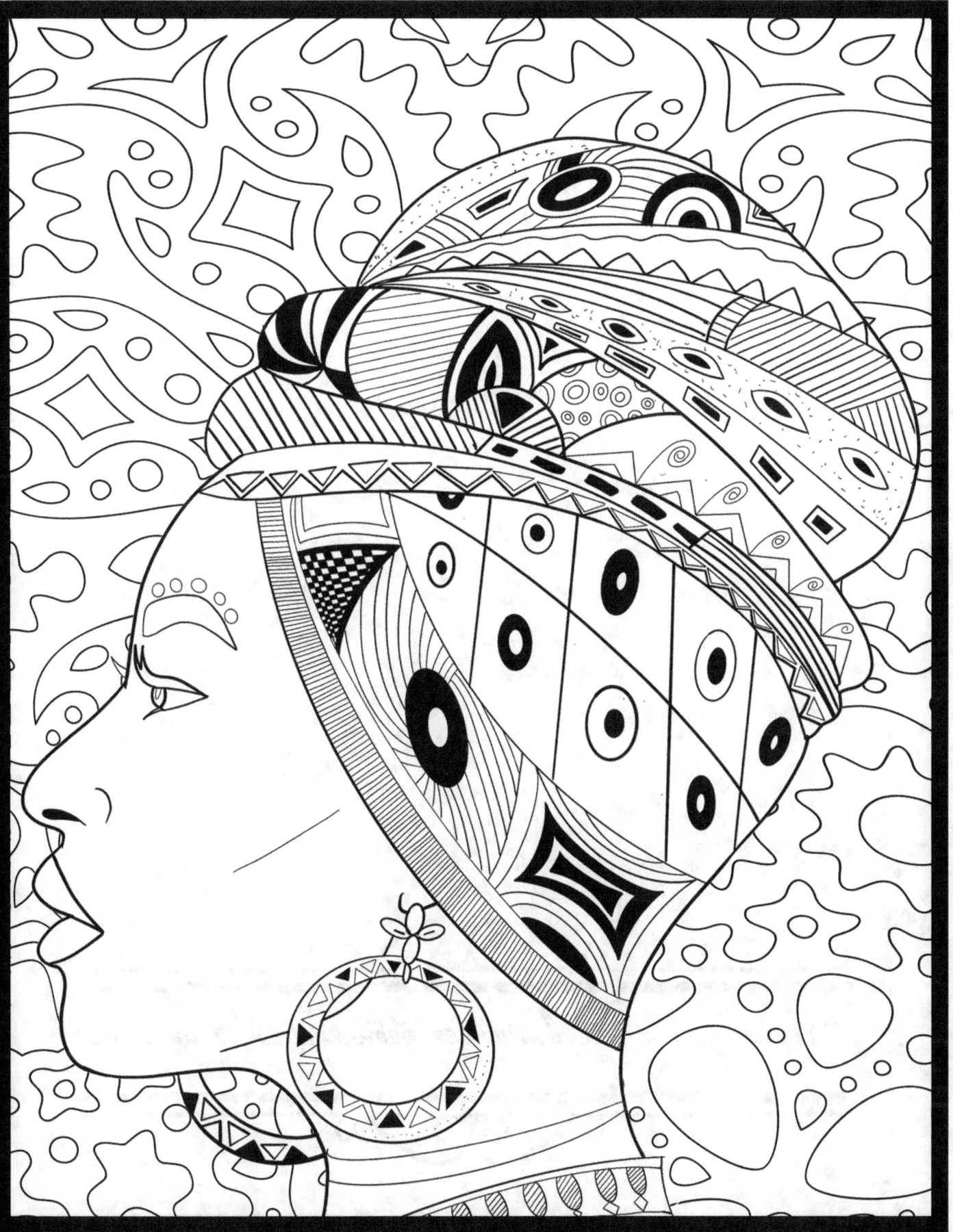

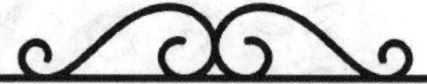

My exquisite female body radiates loving kindness to the world

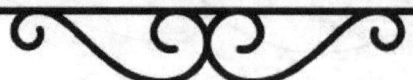

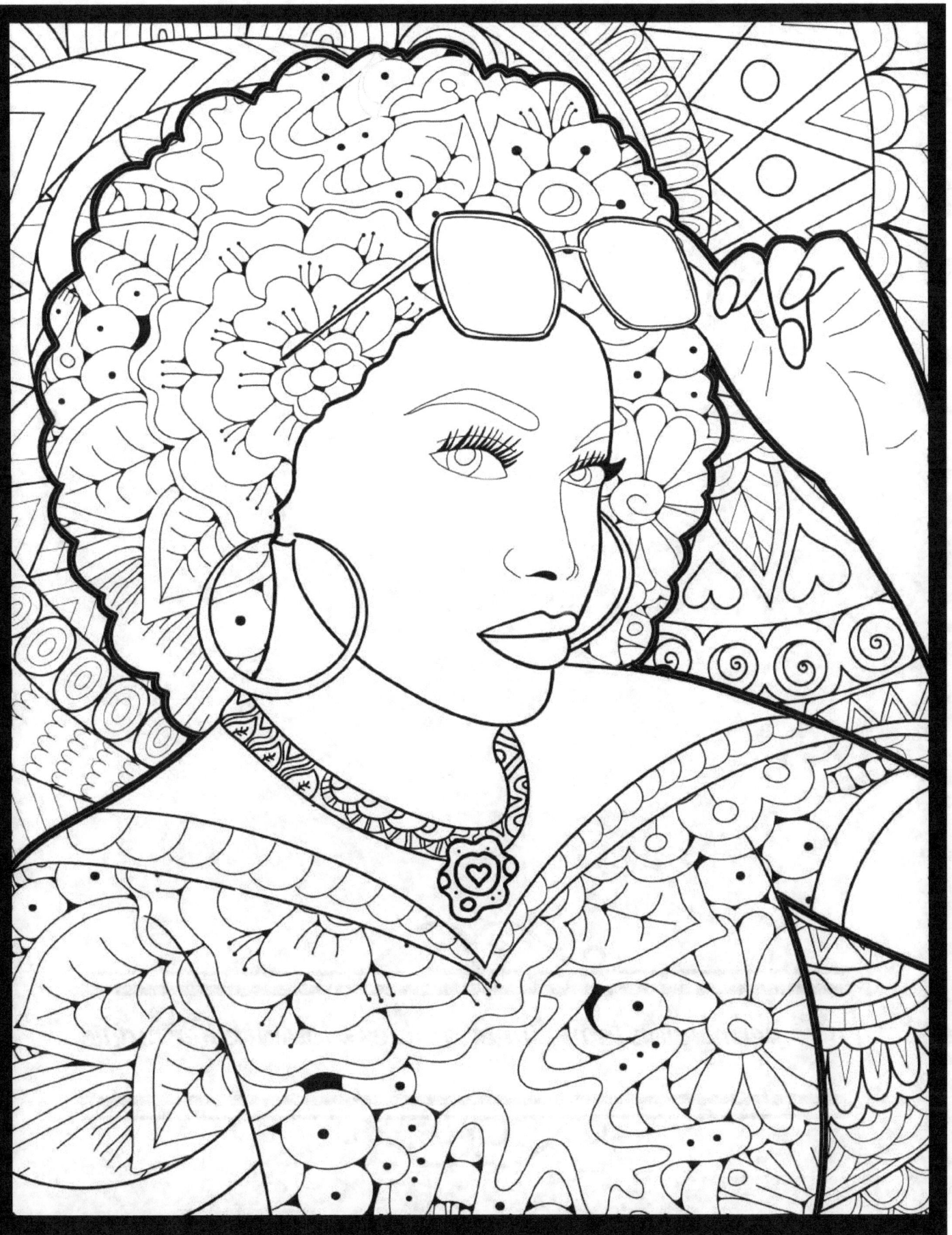

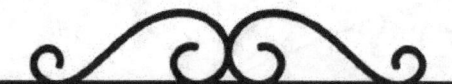

I give permission to my inner goddess to work her magic

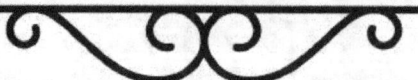

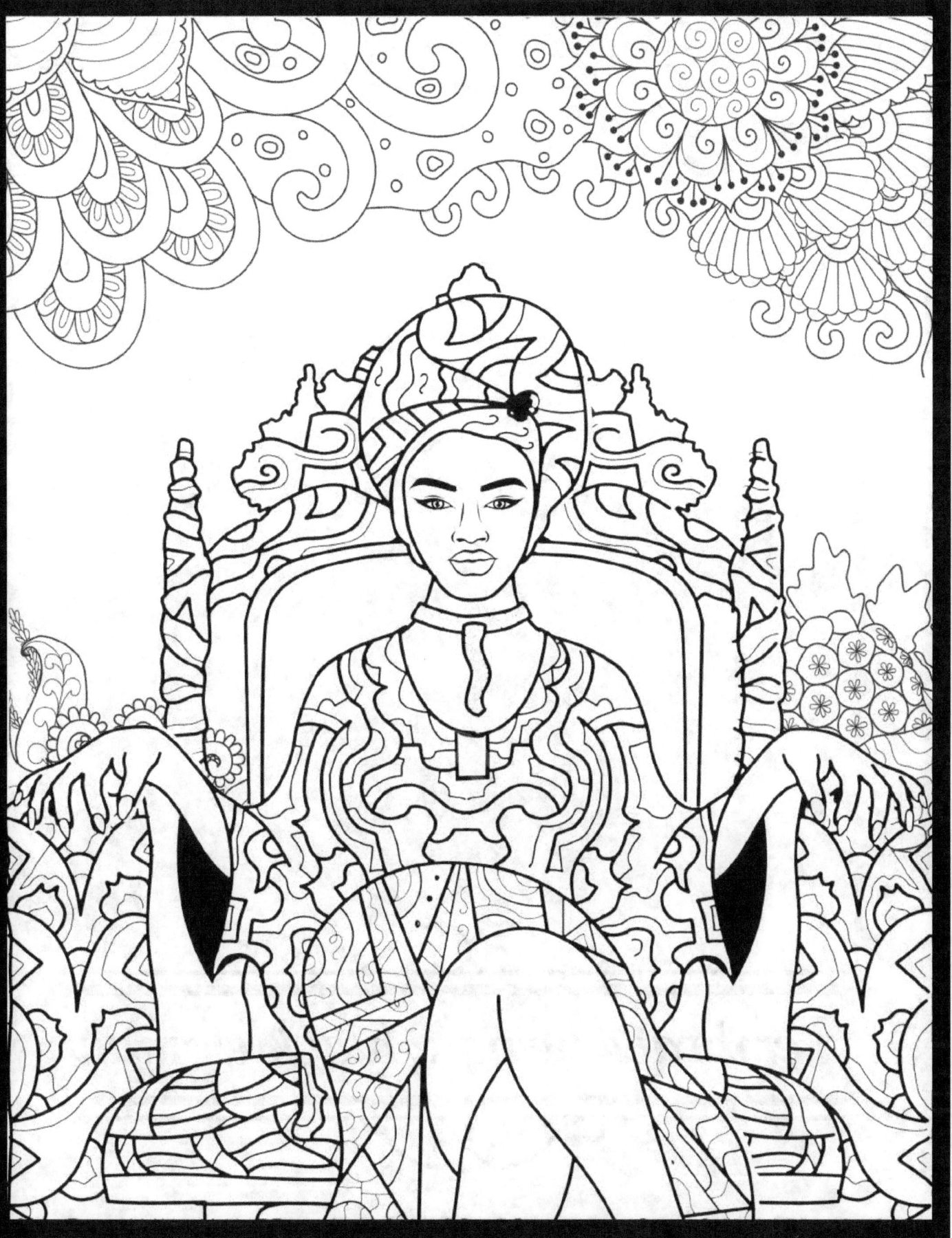

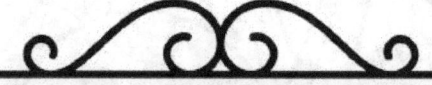

I embrace being a black woman

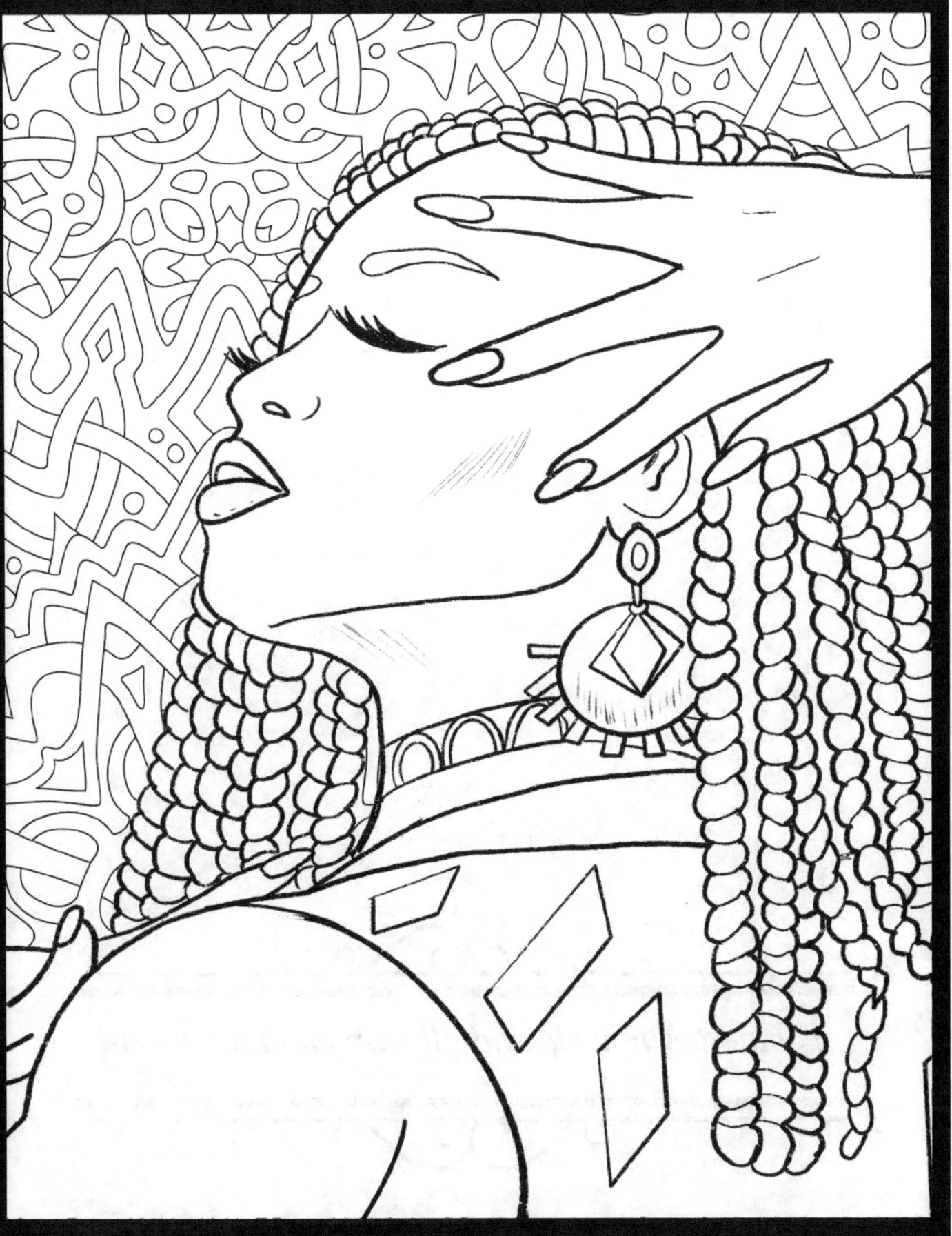

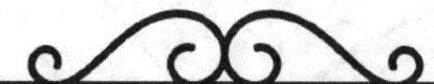

I empower myself and all women in the world

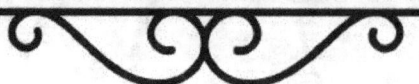

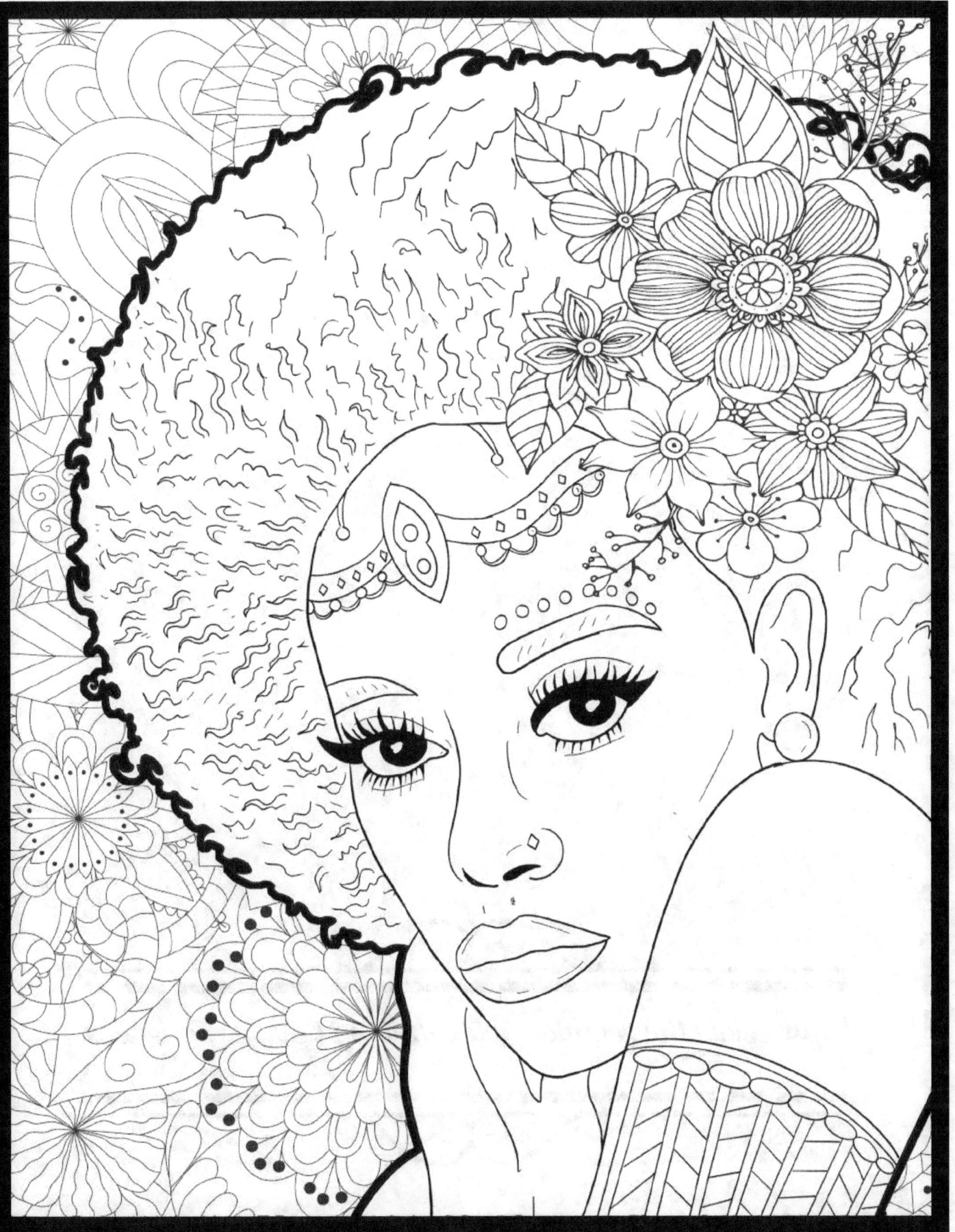

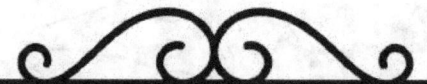

I appreciate the female cycles that my body experiences

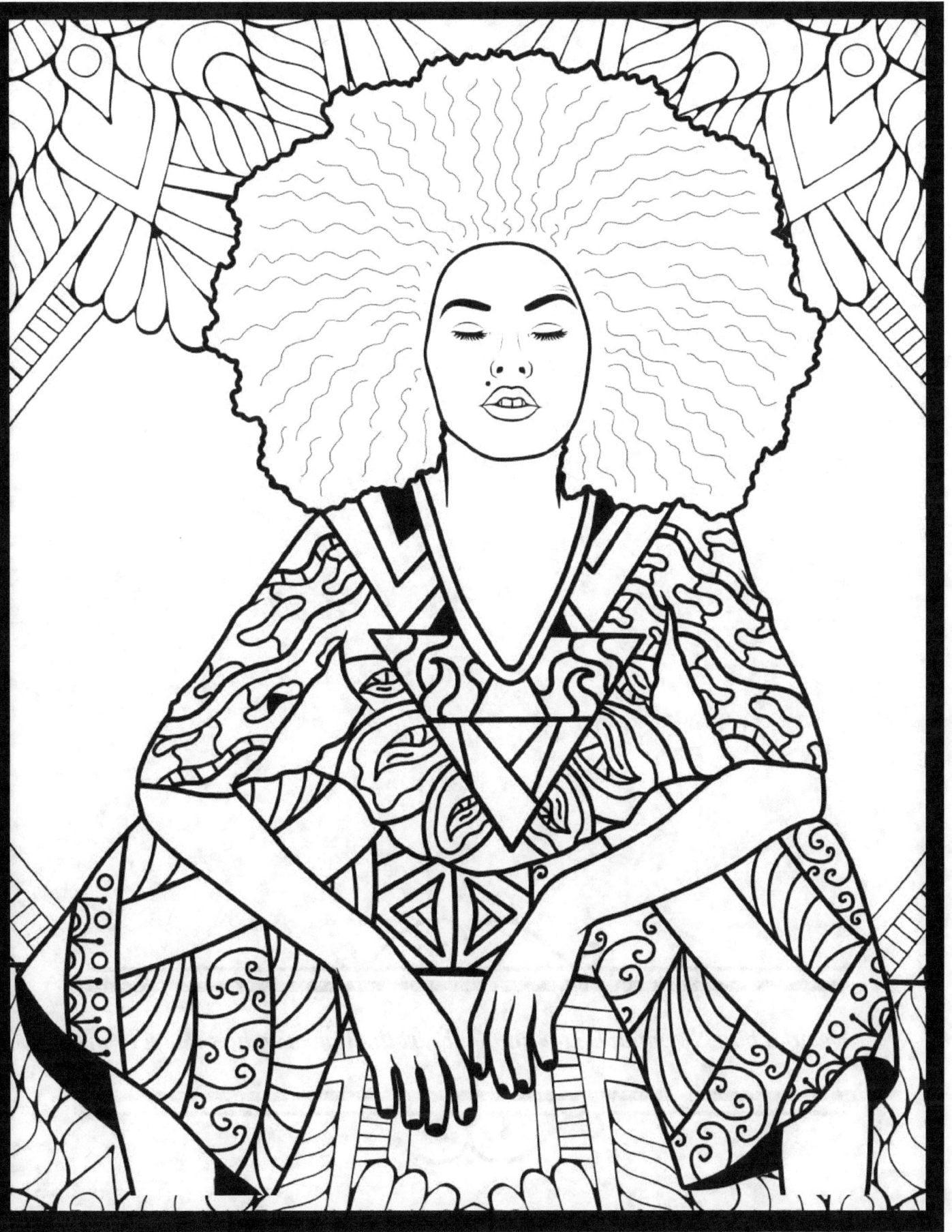

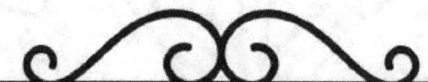

Being a black woman is the greatest gift the universe has given to me

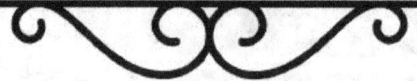

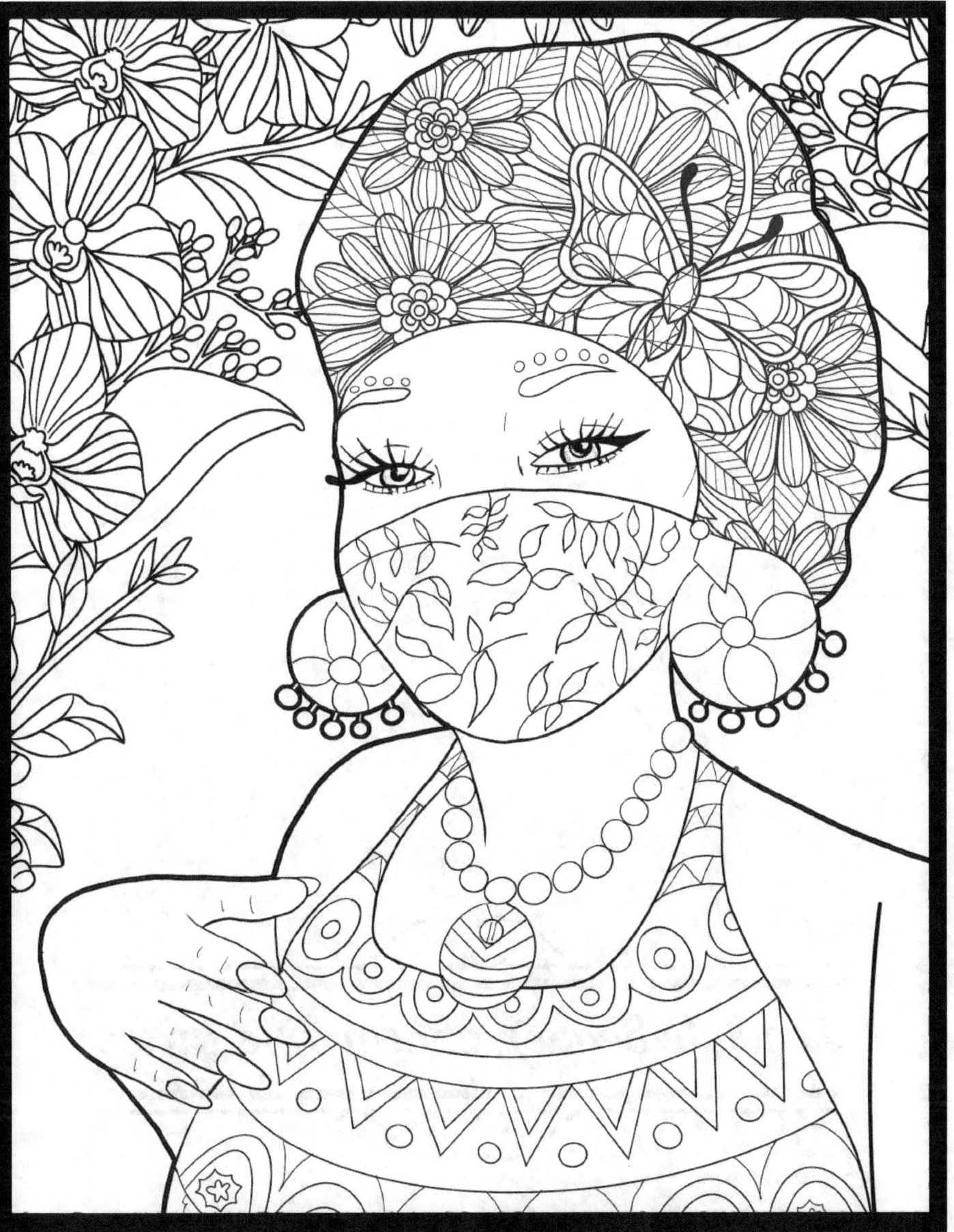

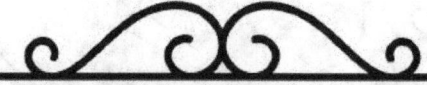

I radiate beauty, charm, and grace

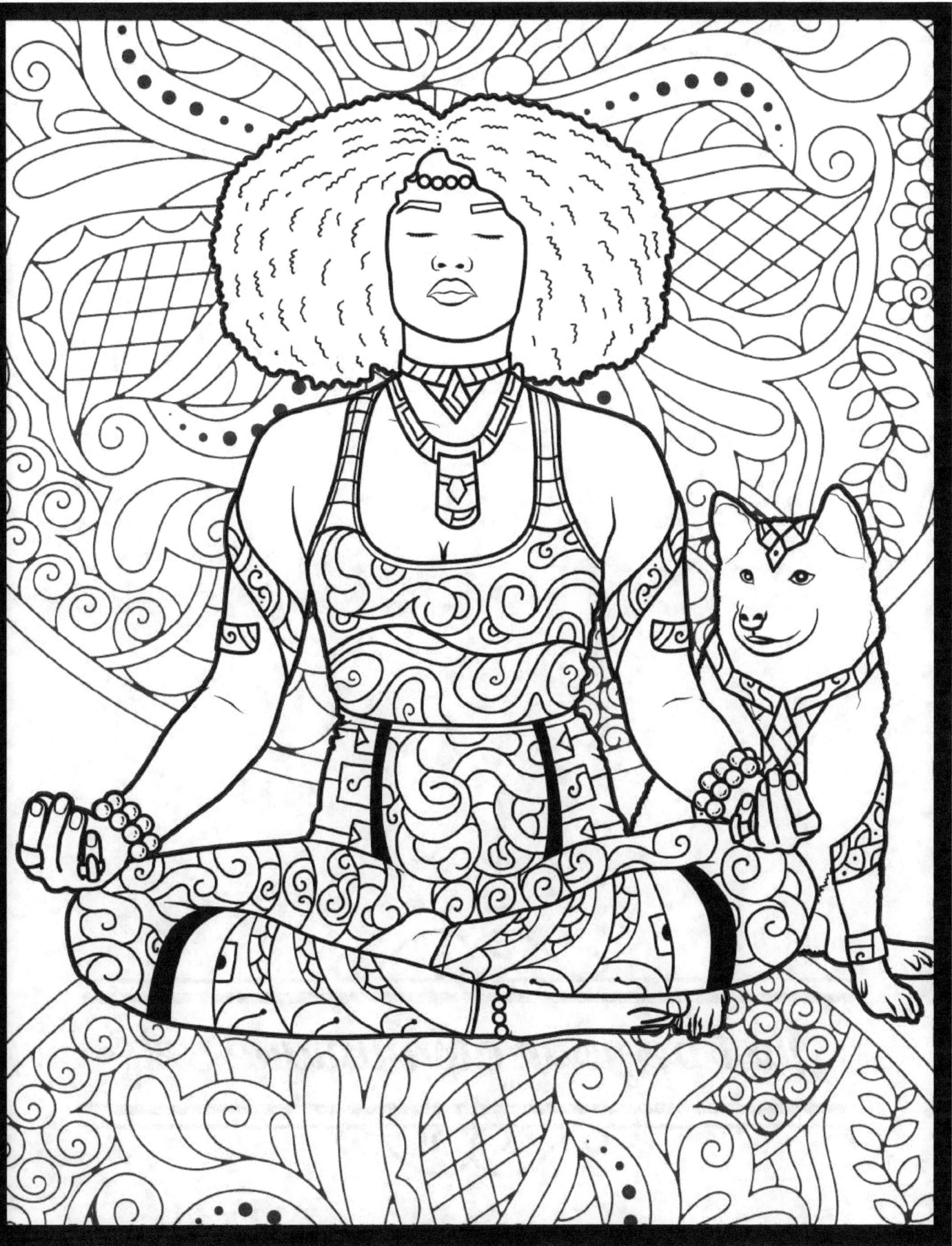

Just be your own unique self

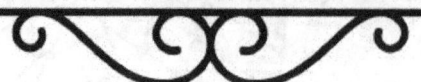

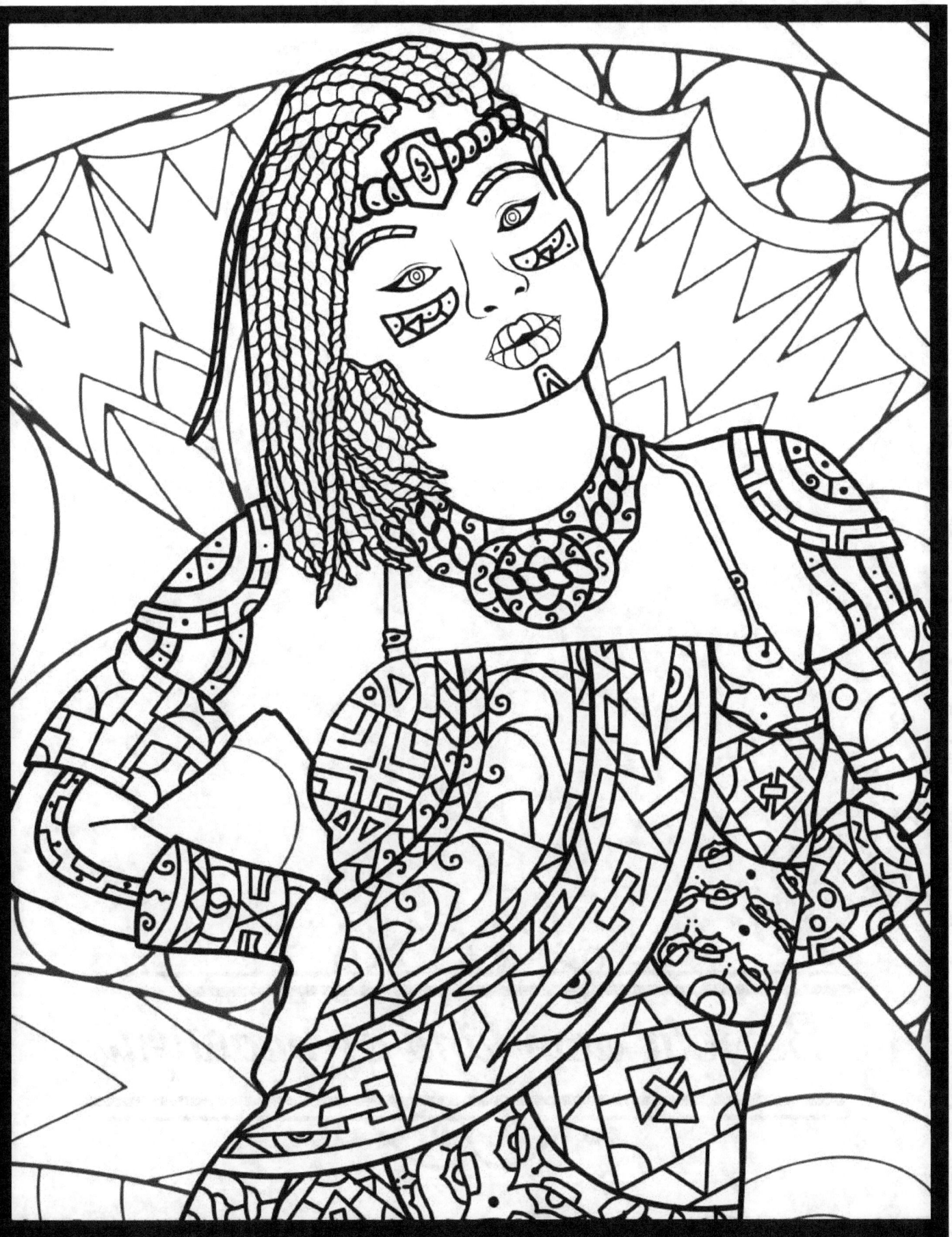

Be your own kind of beautiful

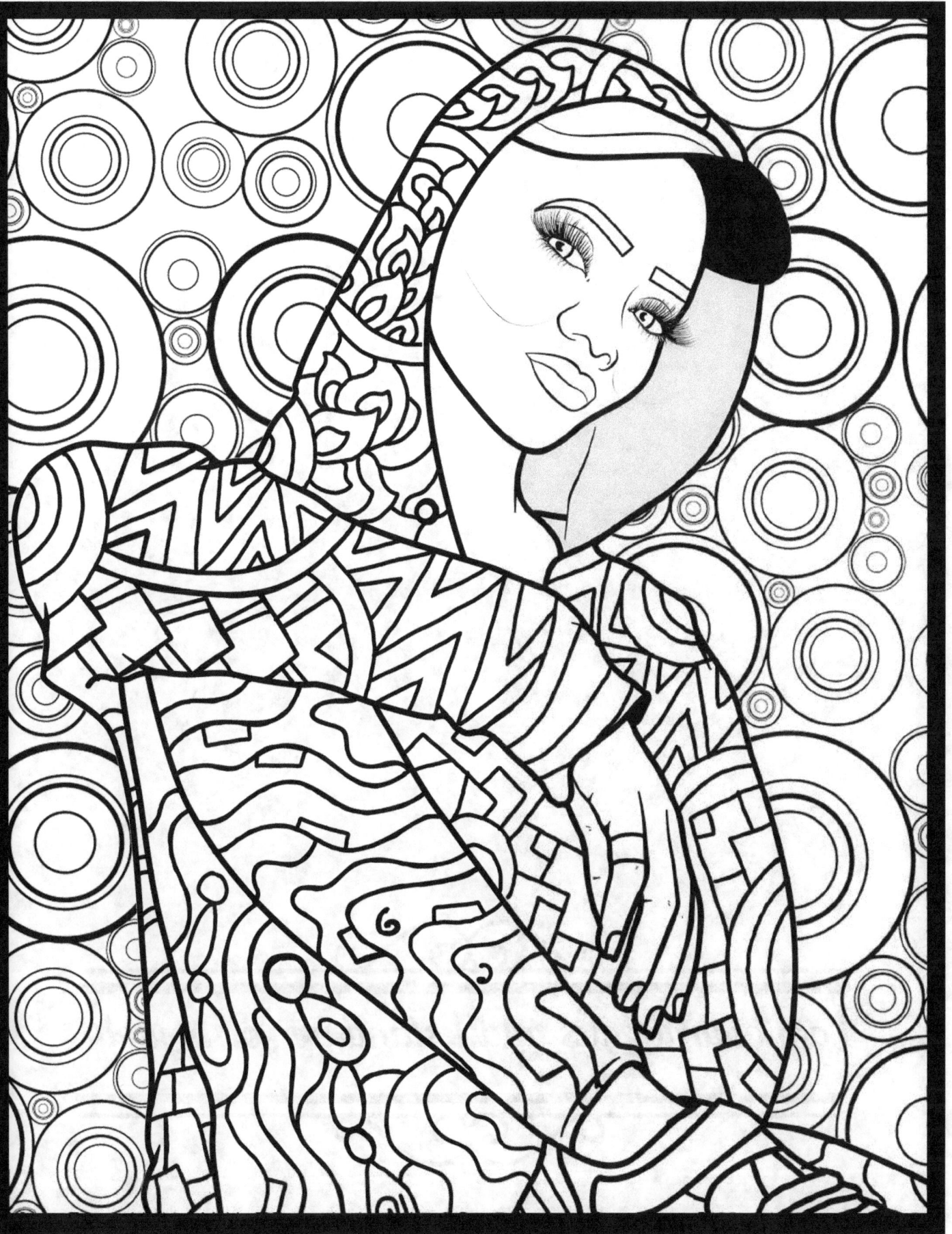

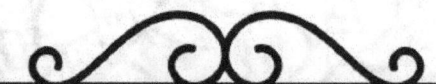

I am courageous and I stand up for myself

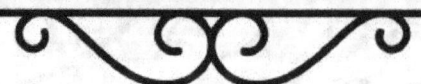

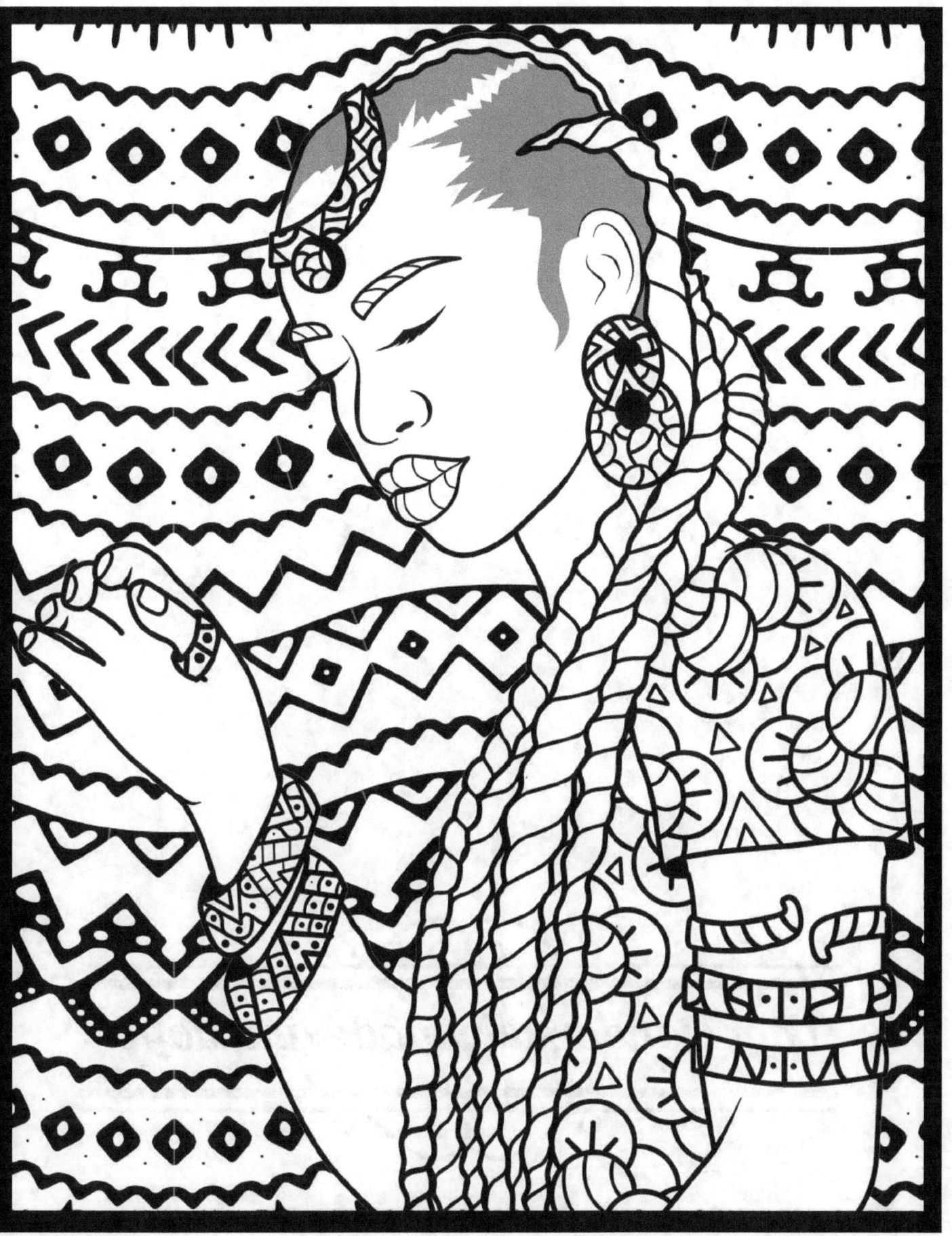

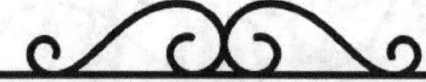

I am wonderfully made and dope

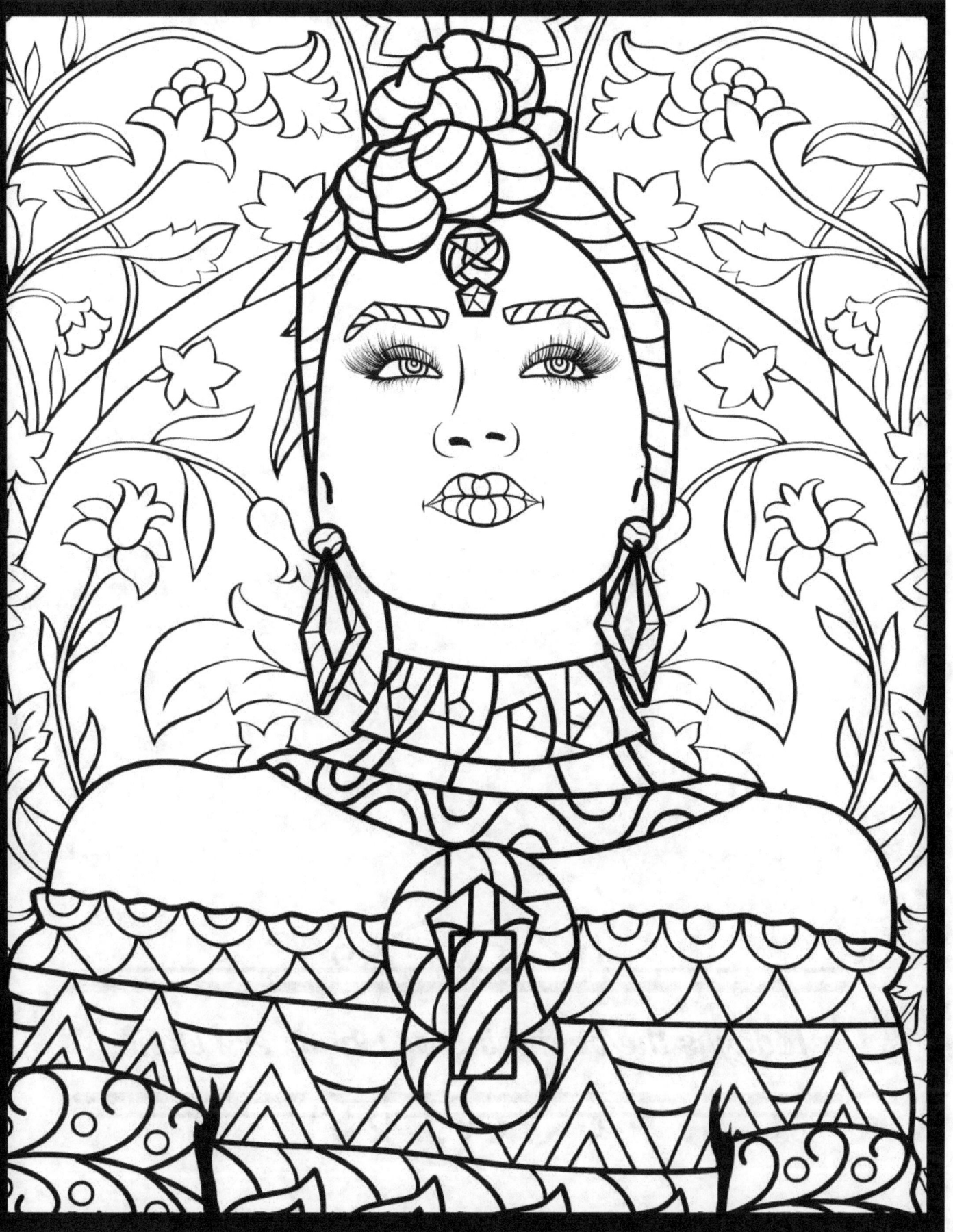

Today is the beginning of whatever I want

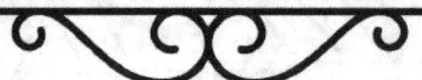

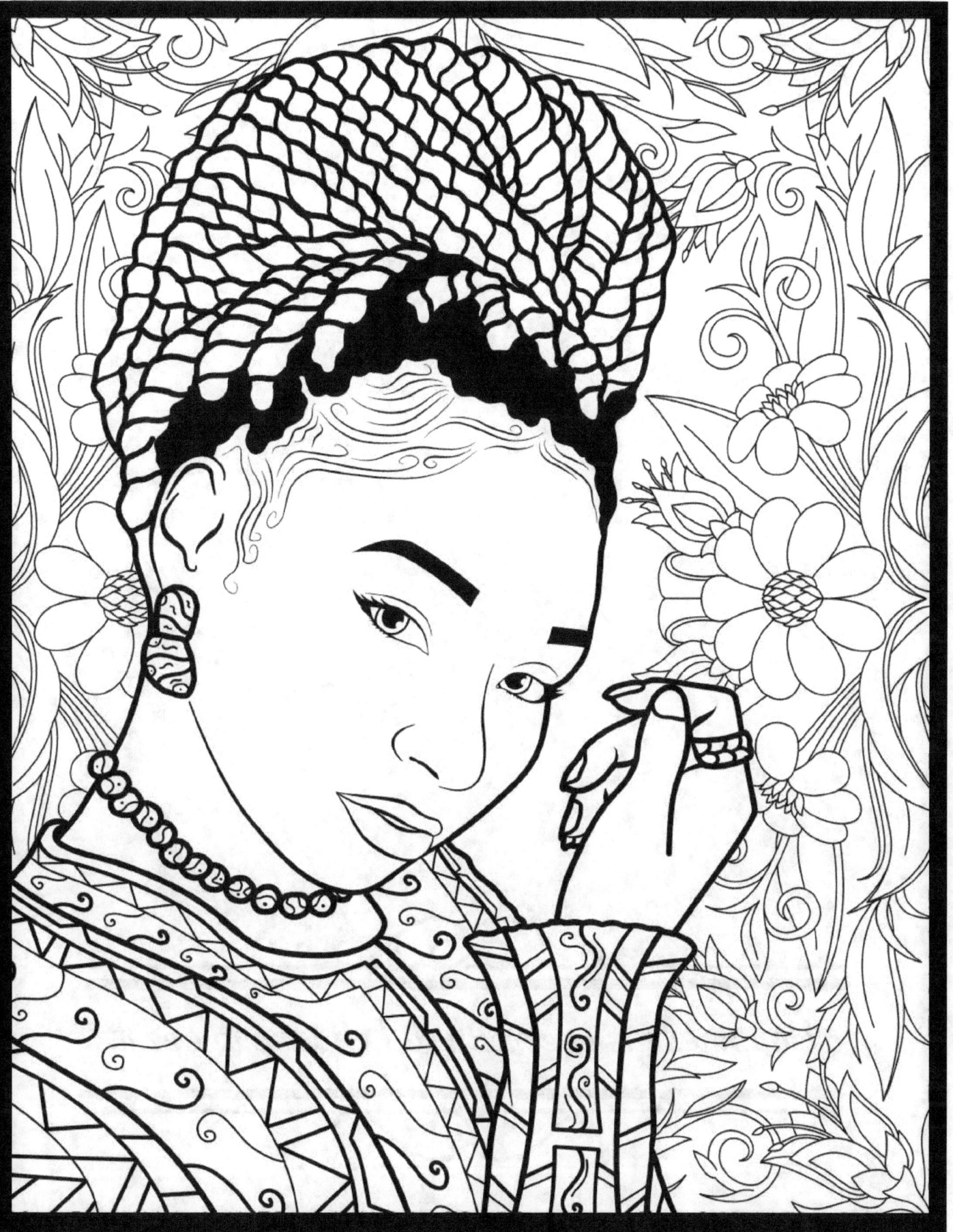

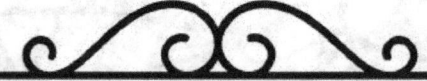

Happiness is everywhere I choose to see it

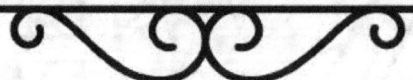

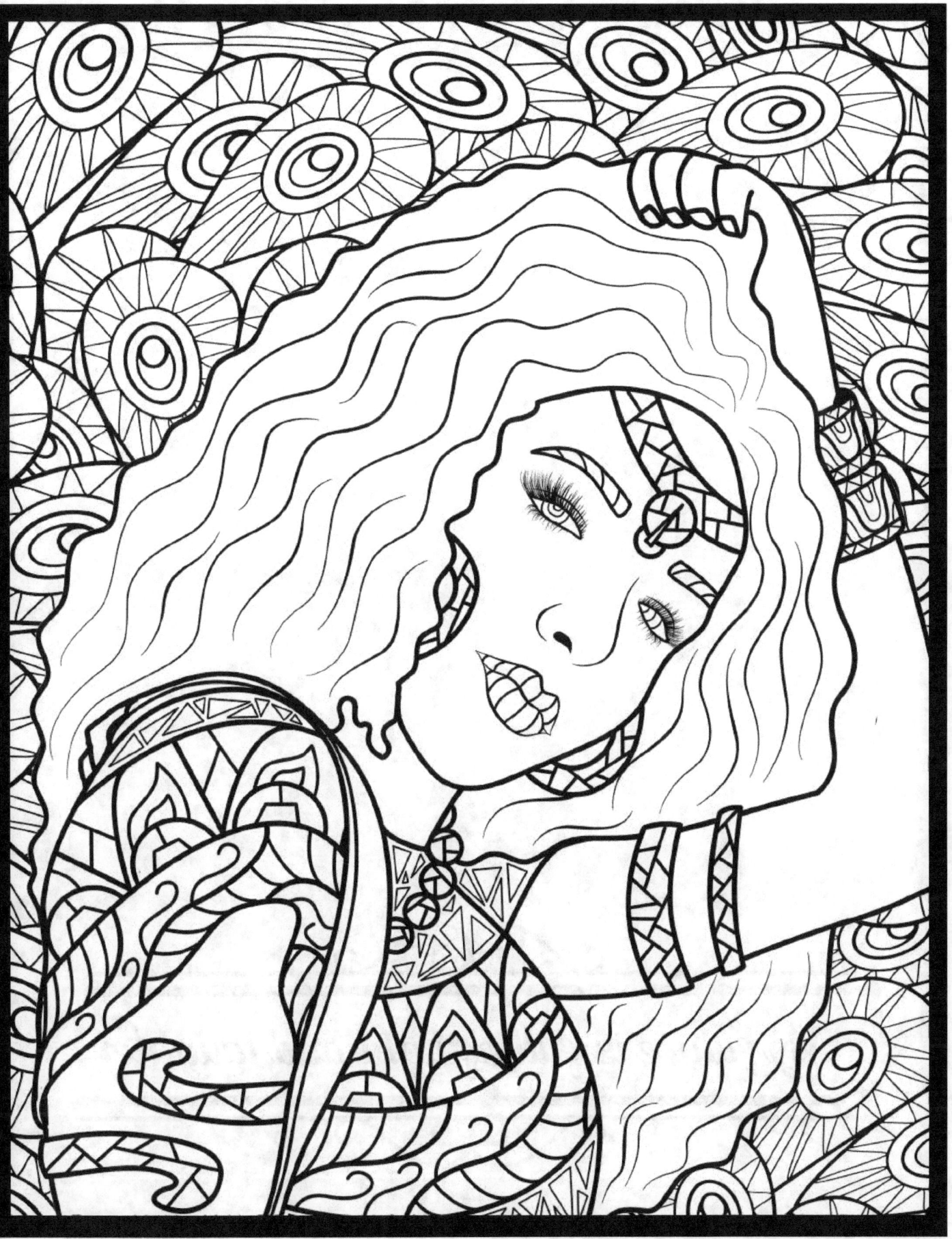

My future is full of light and laughter

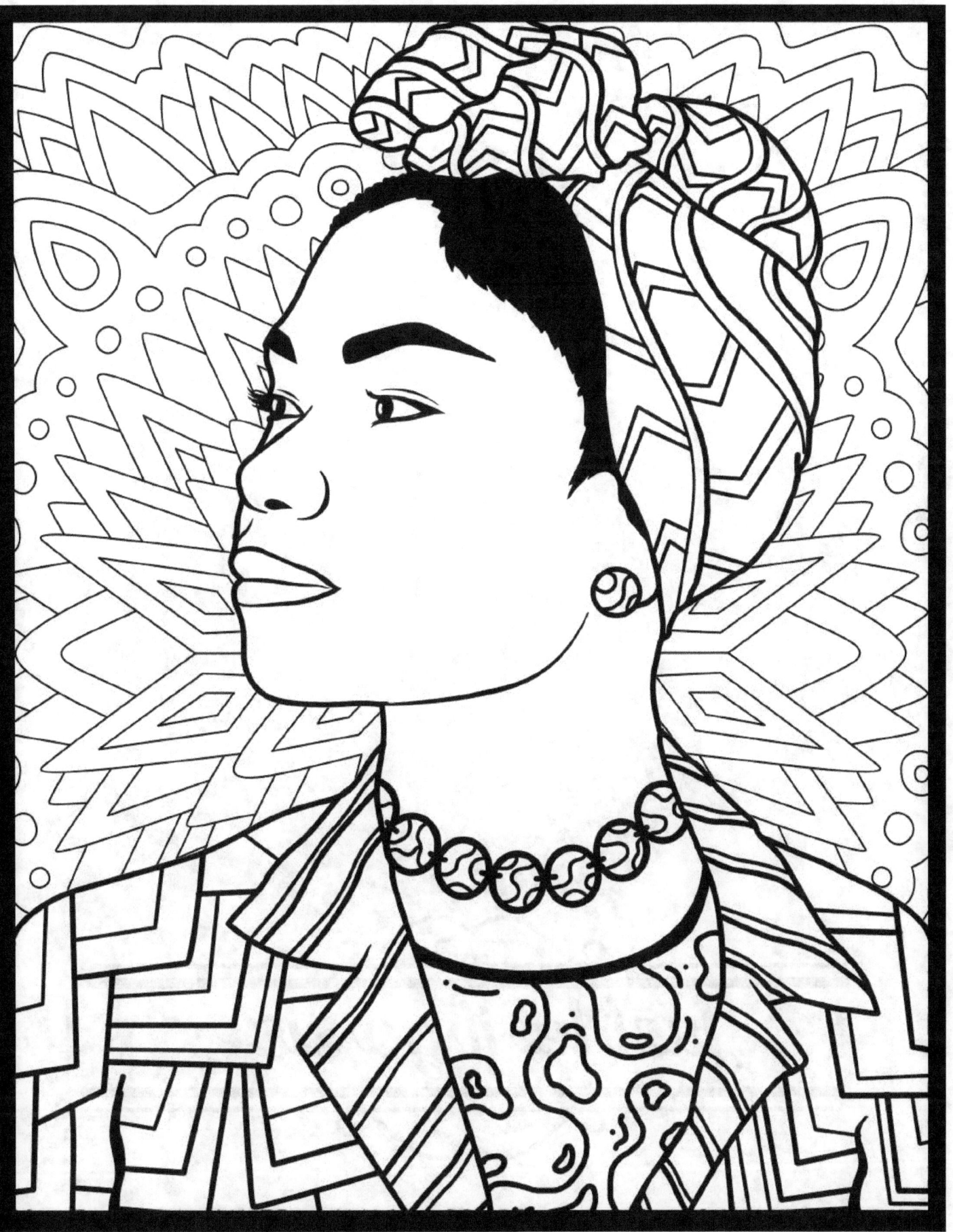

Just let it go sis

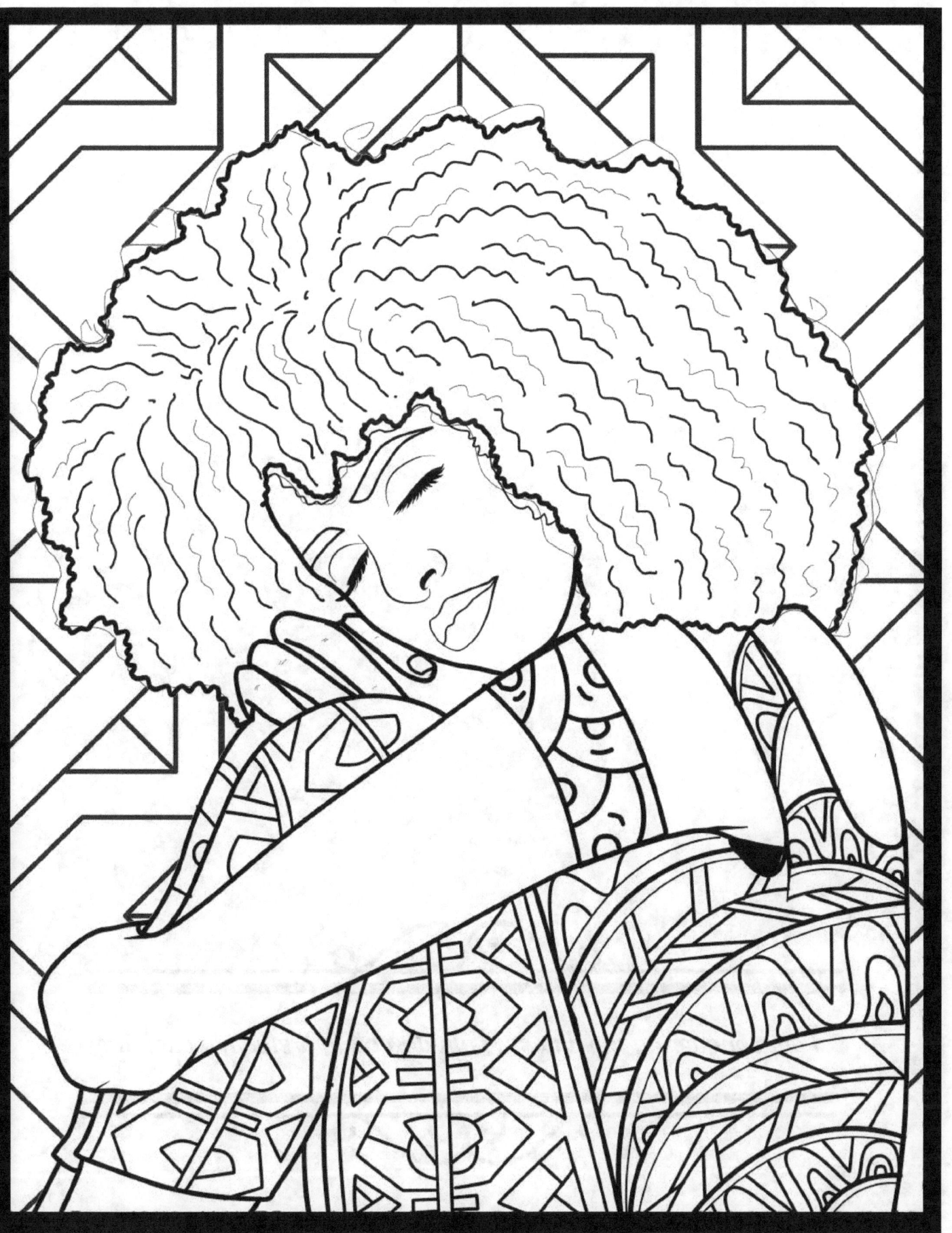

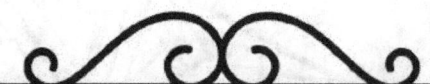

I am conquering my illness; I am defeating it steadily each day

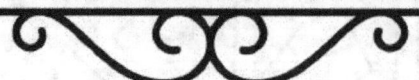

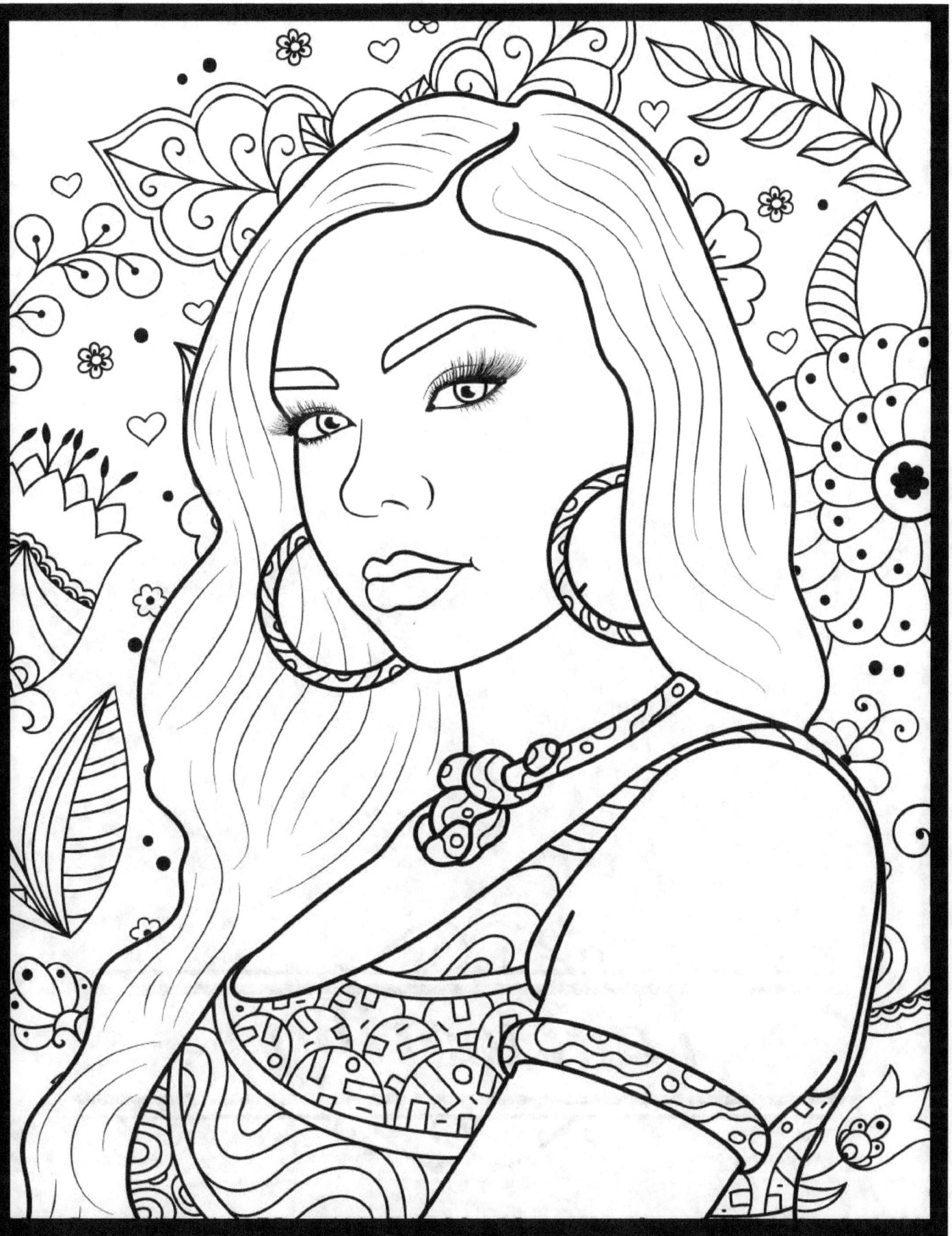

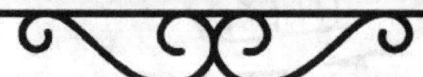
I am worthy

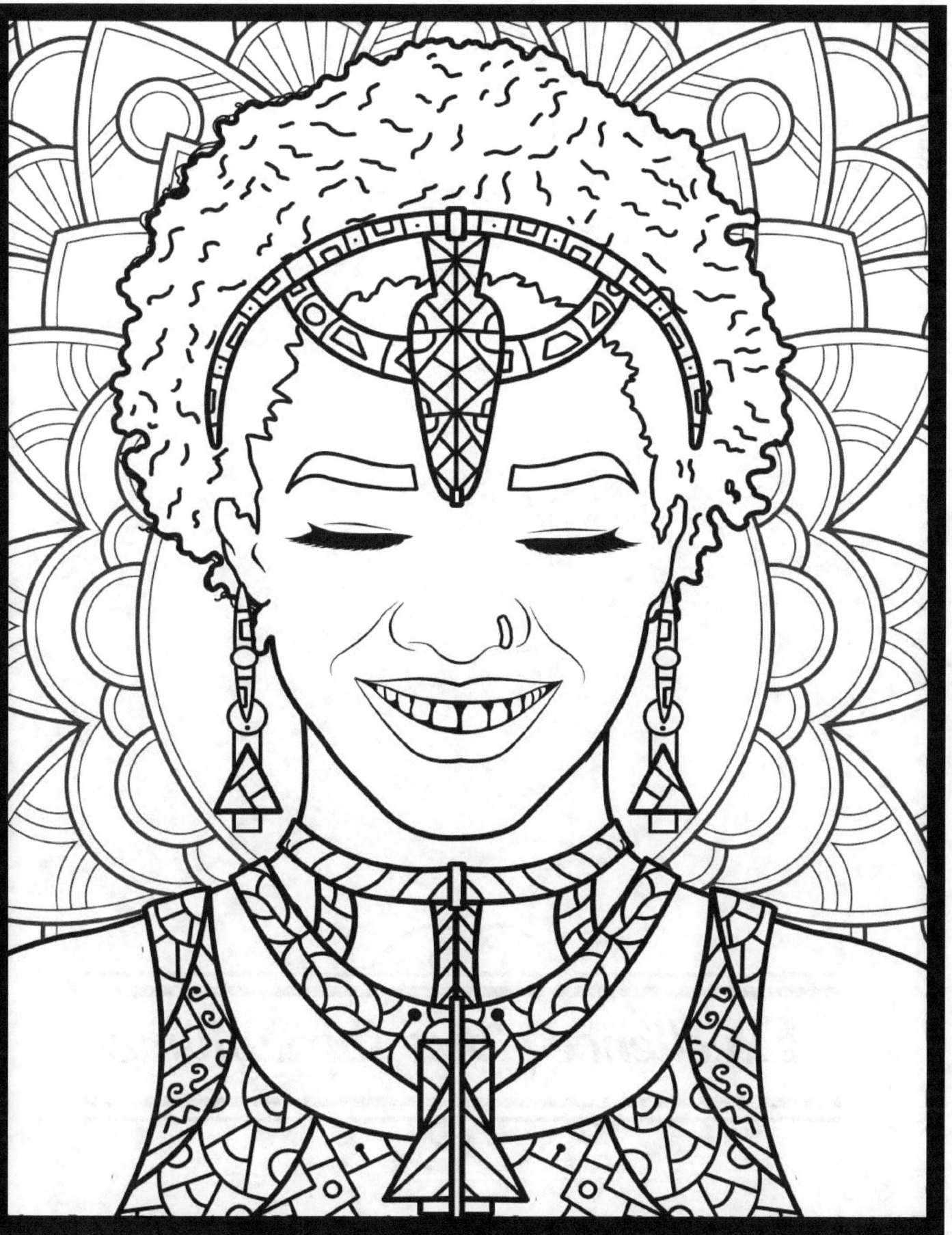

Excellence flows through me

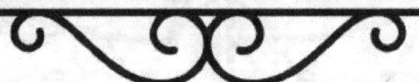

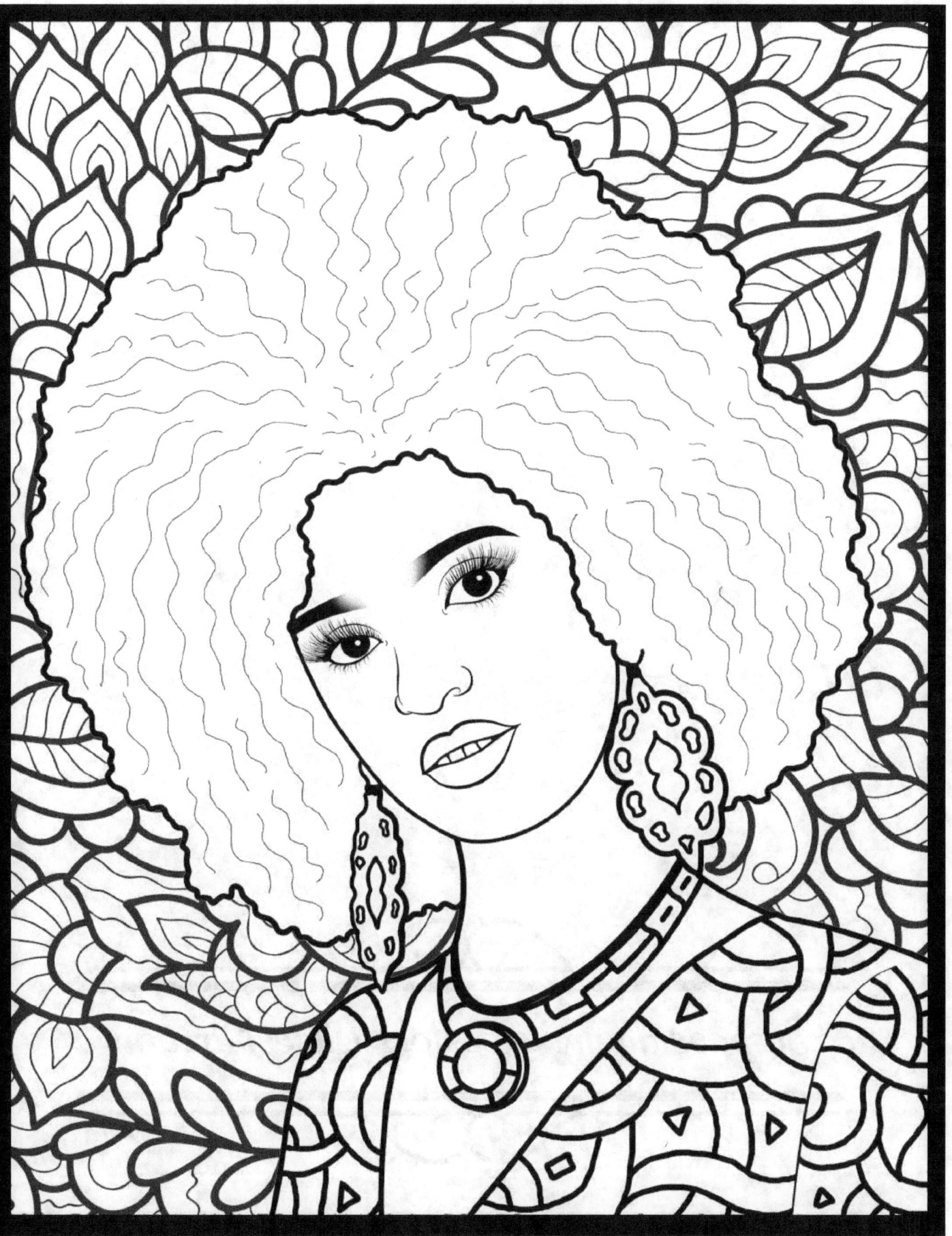

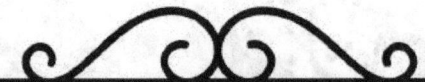

Surpassing my ancestors wildest dreams

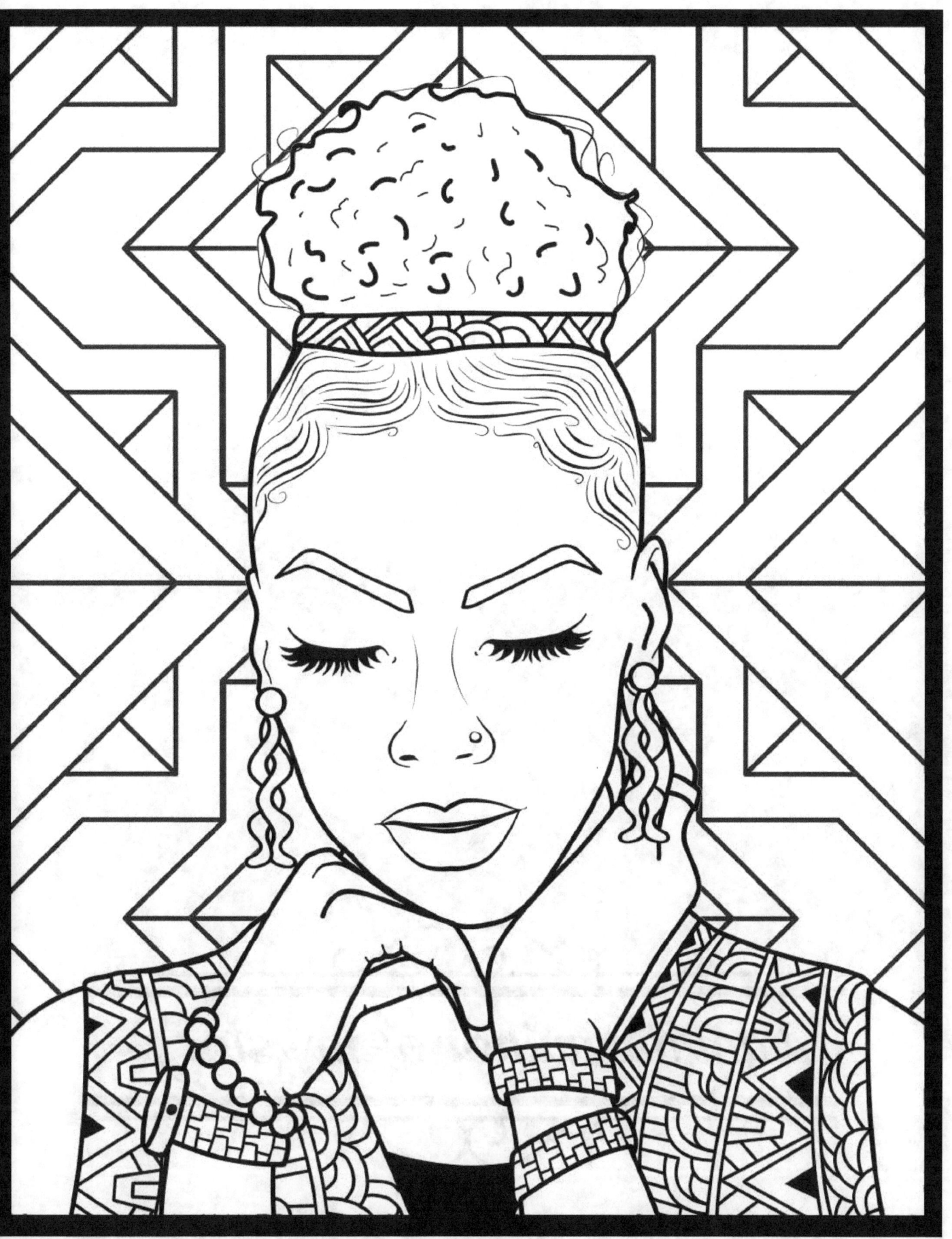

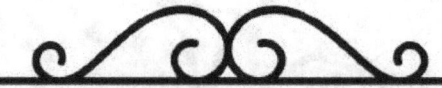

I am the author of my story

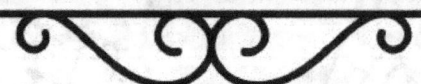

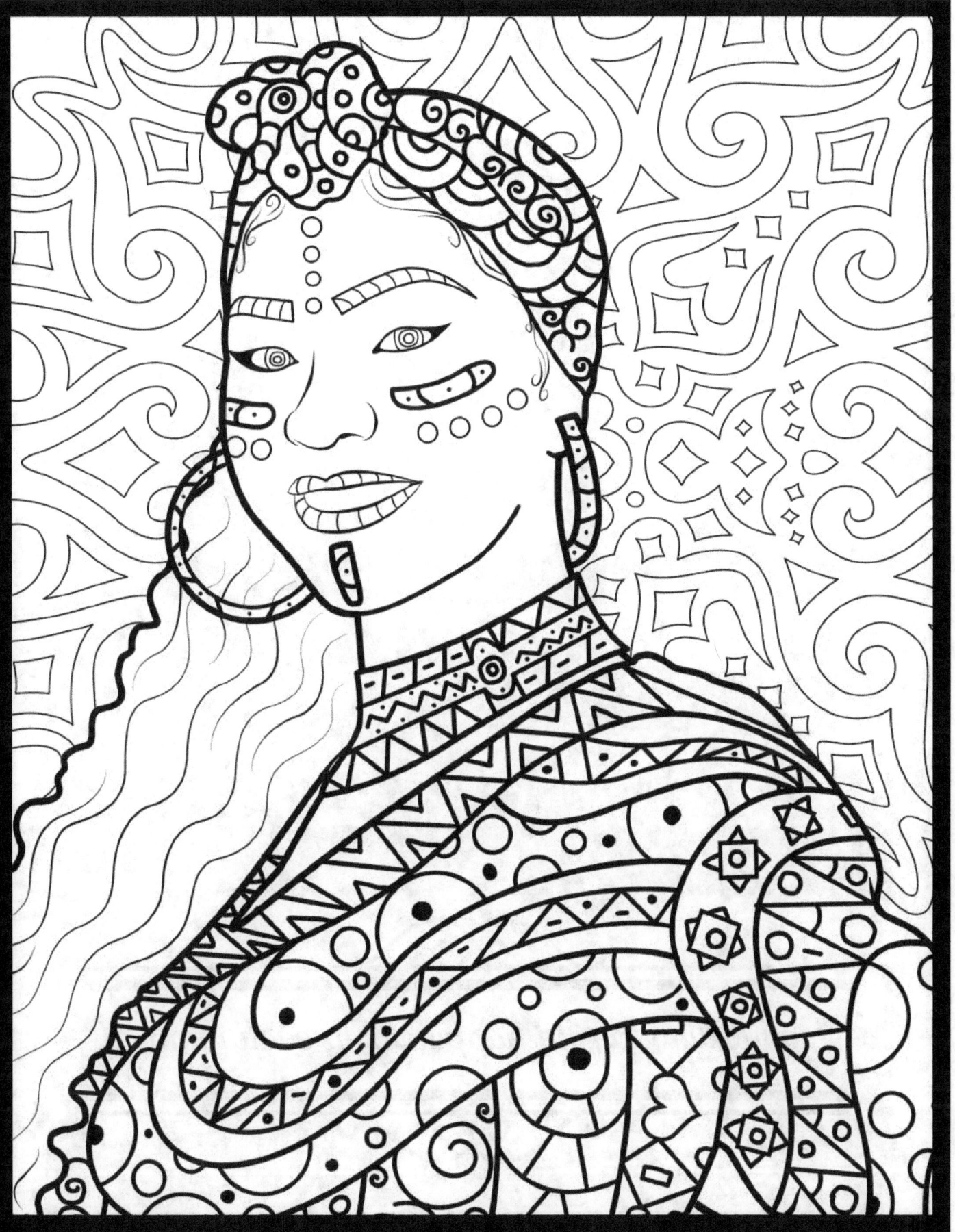

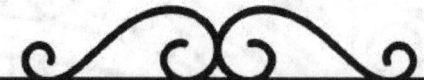

I am willing to find happiness in each moment

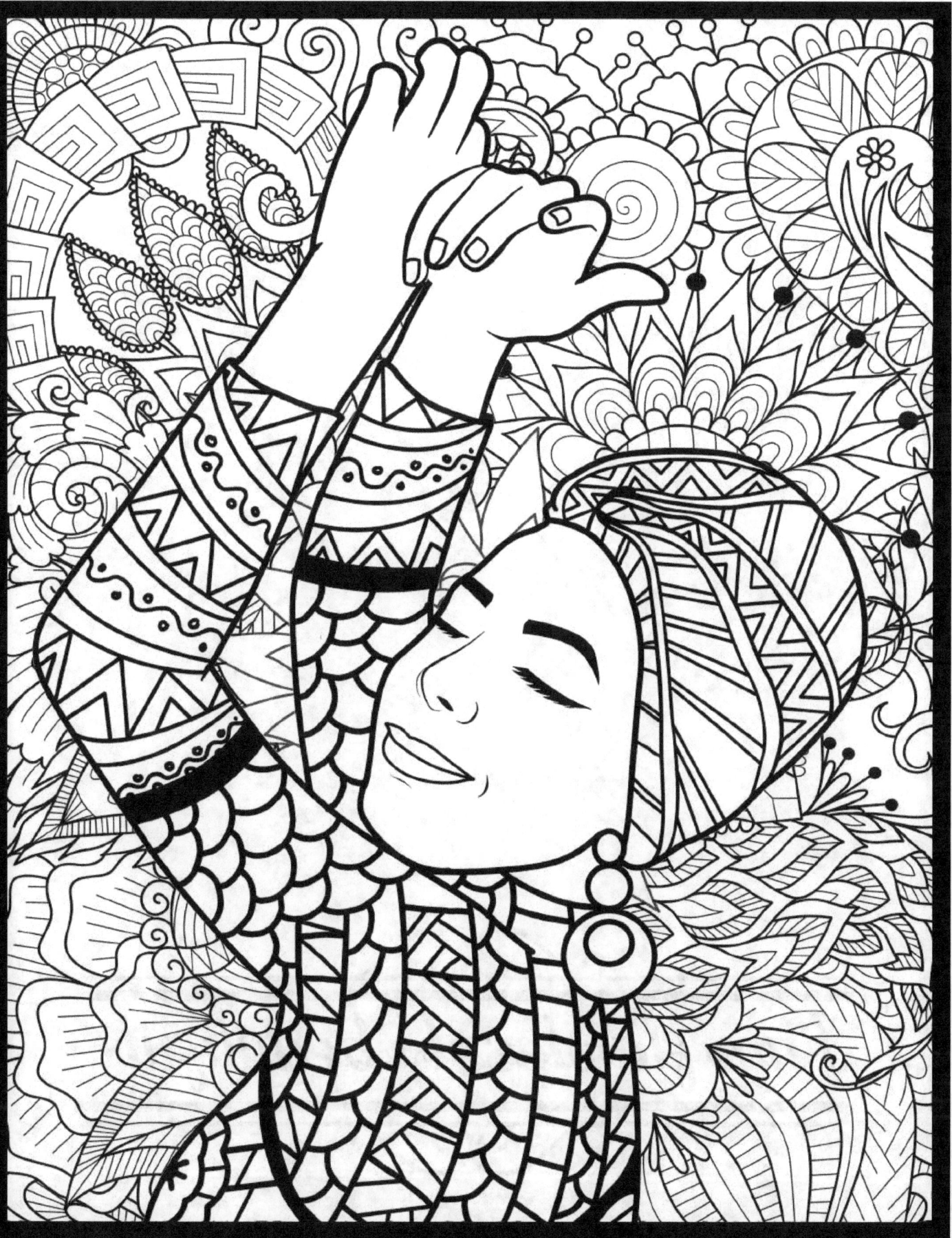

I am flawlessly beautiful

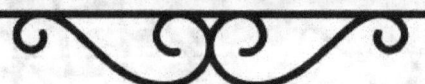

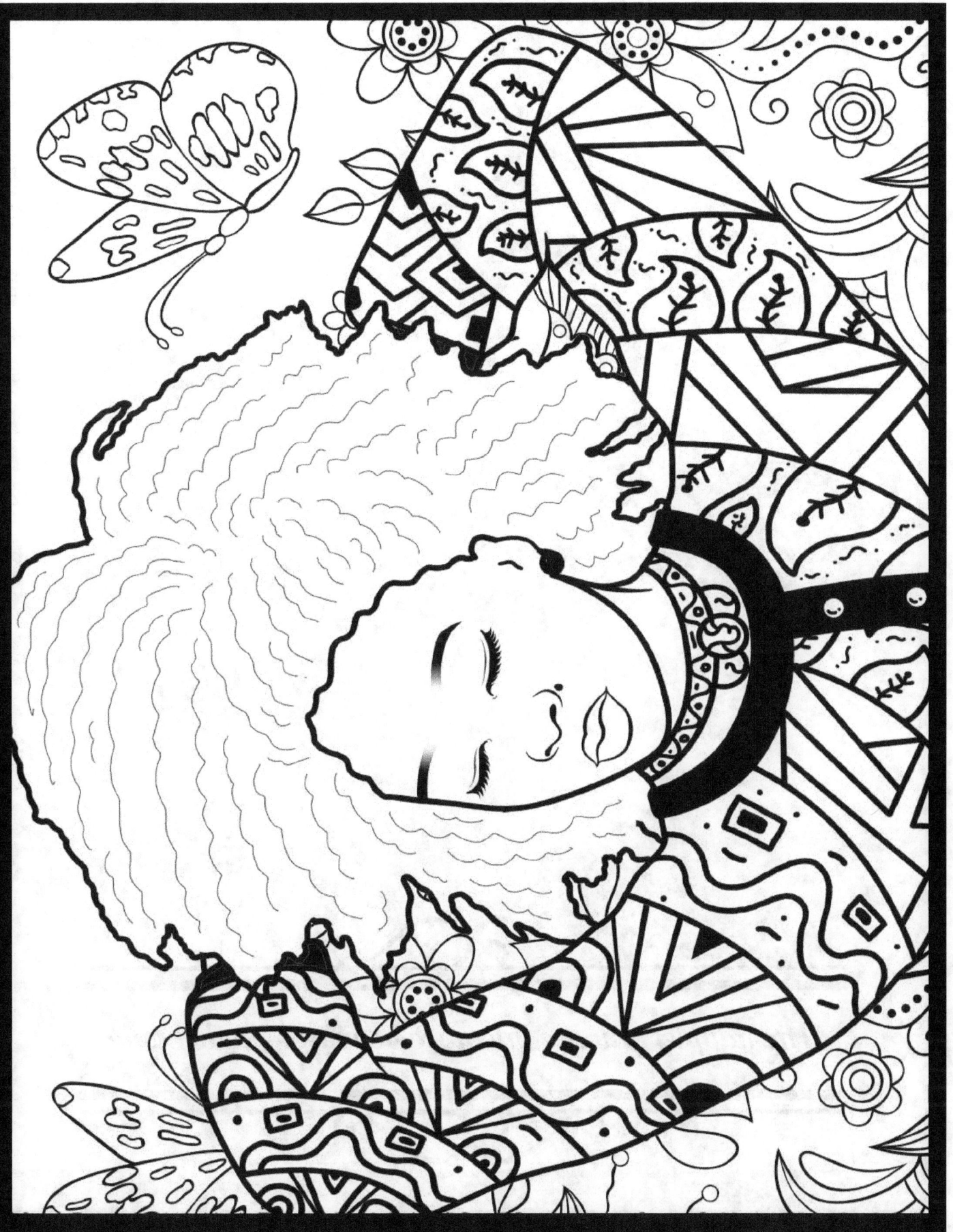

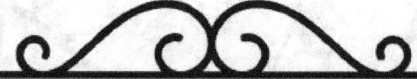

The happier you are the more beautiful you become

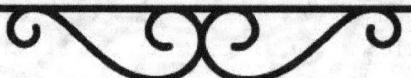

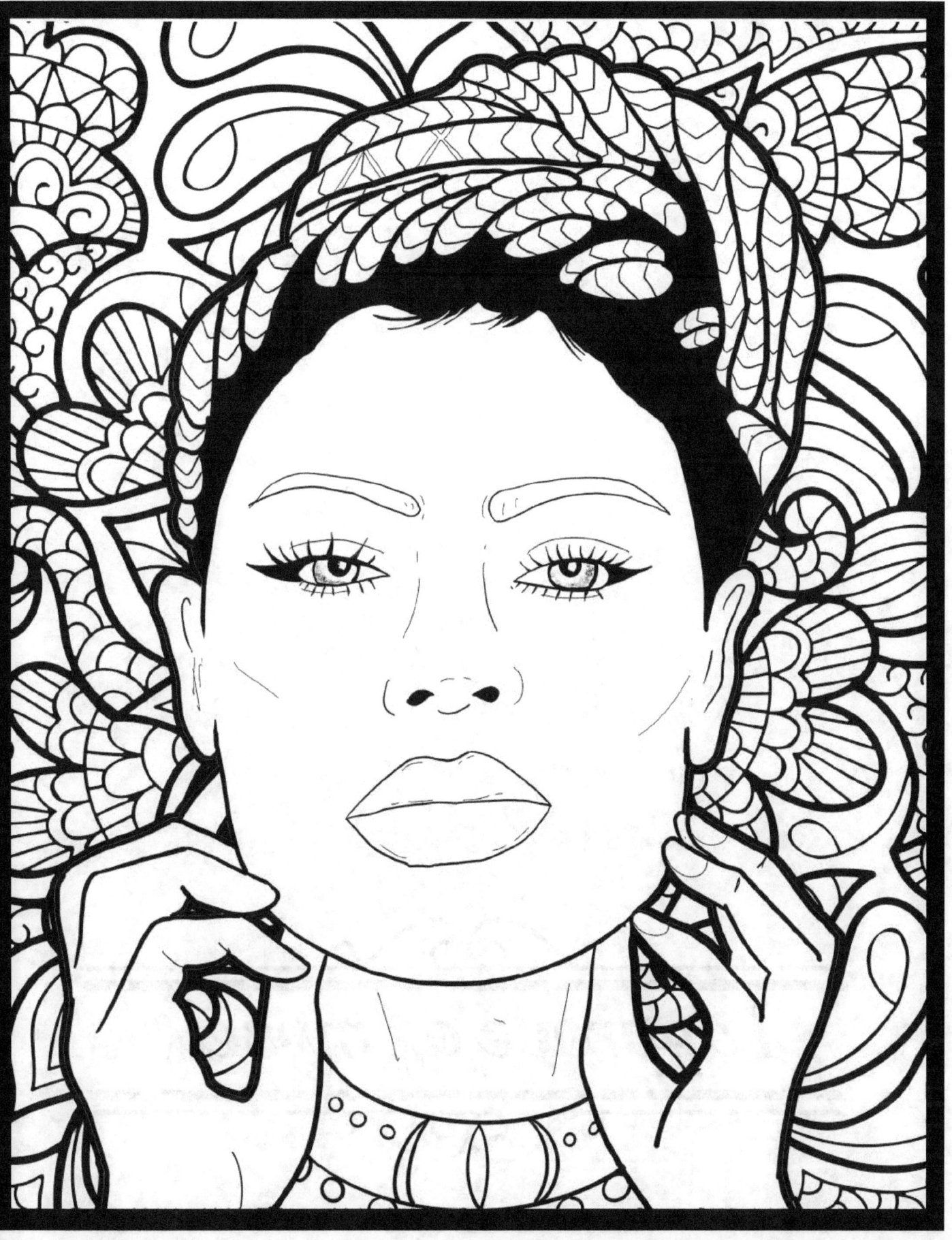

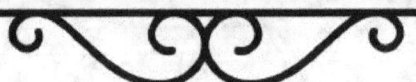

I approve of myself

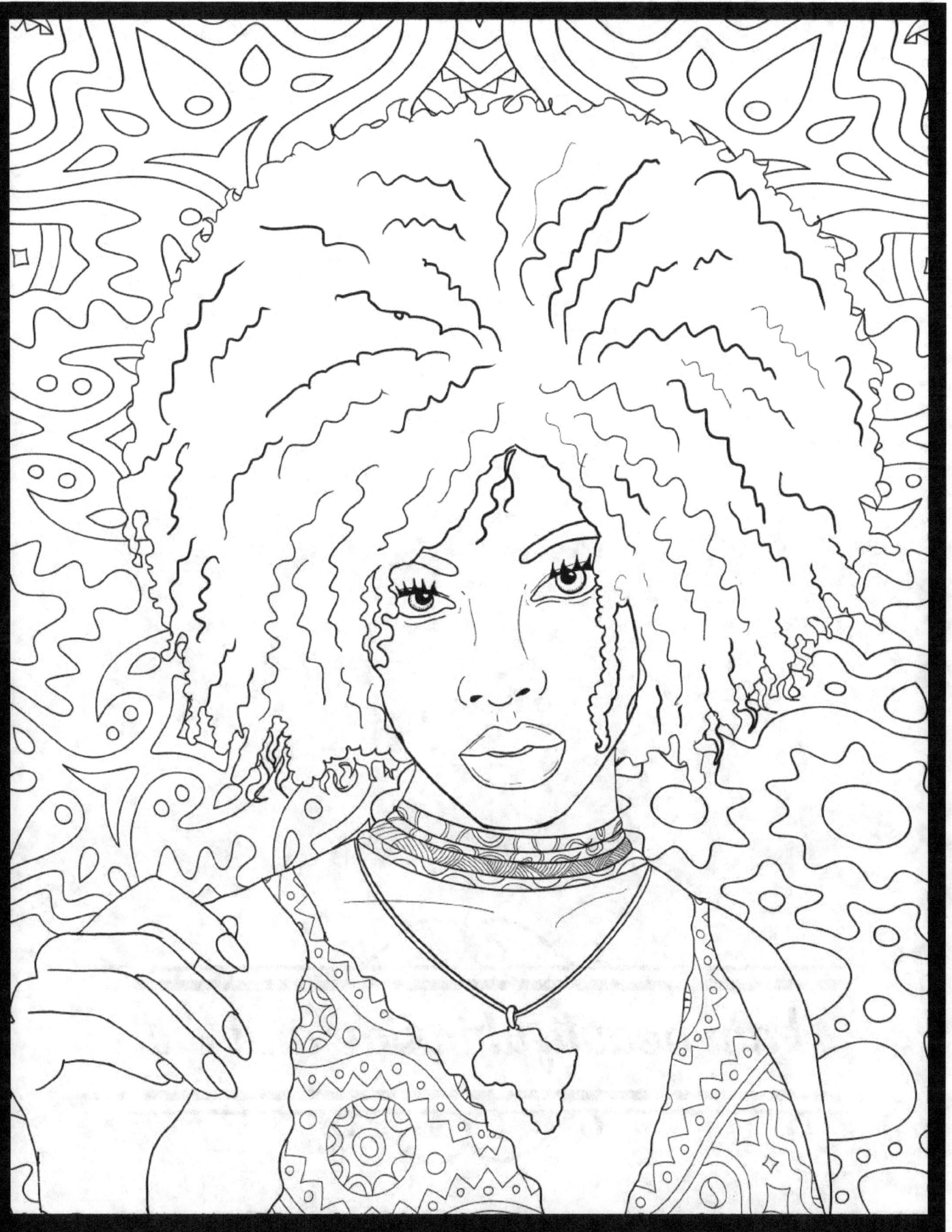

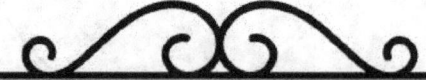

I am beautiful inside and out

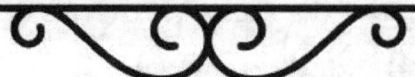

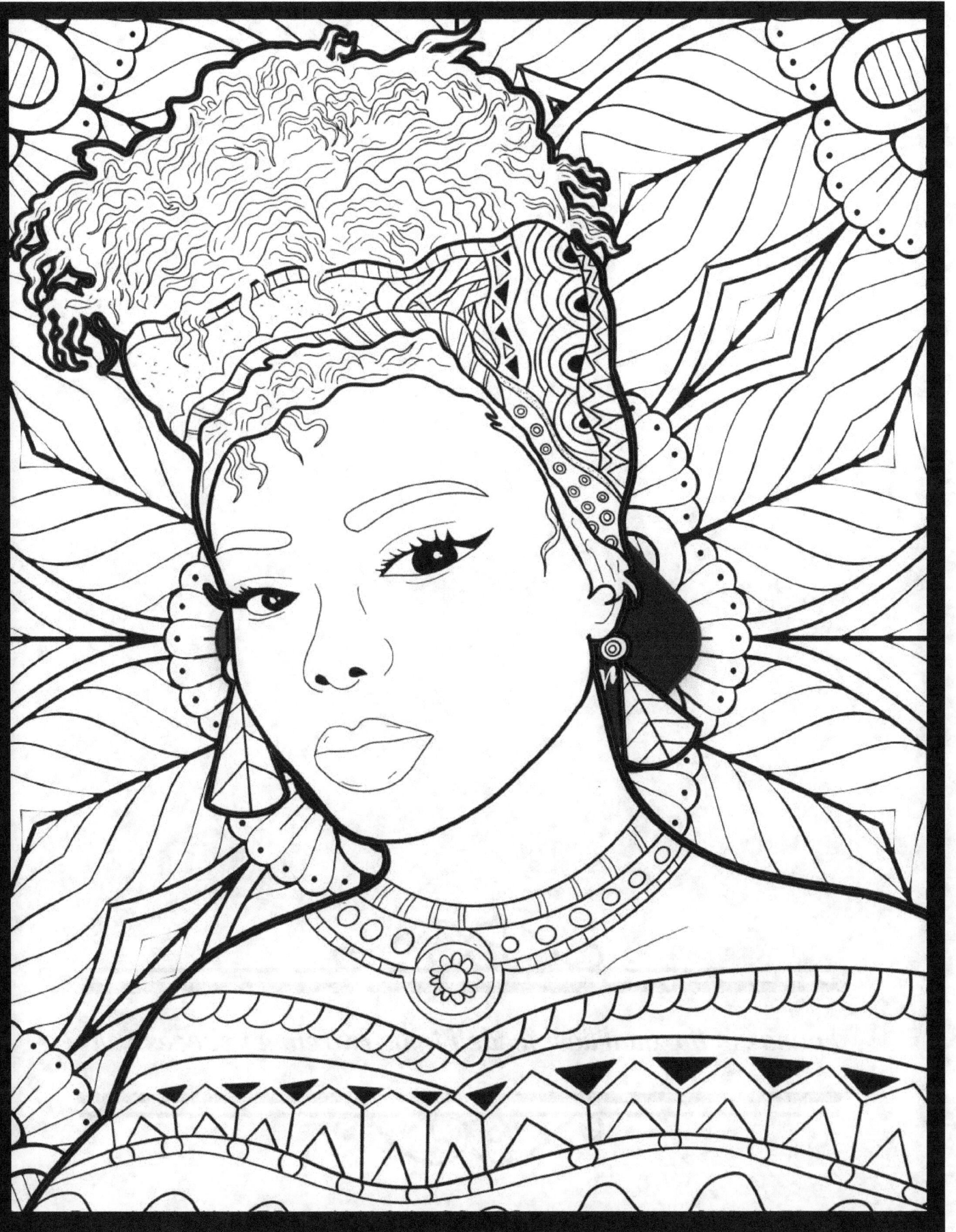

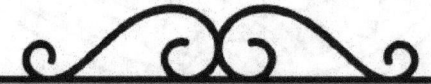

I possess the qualities needed to be extremely successful

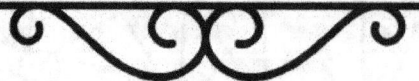

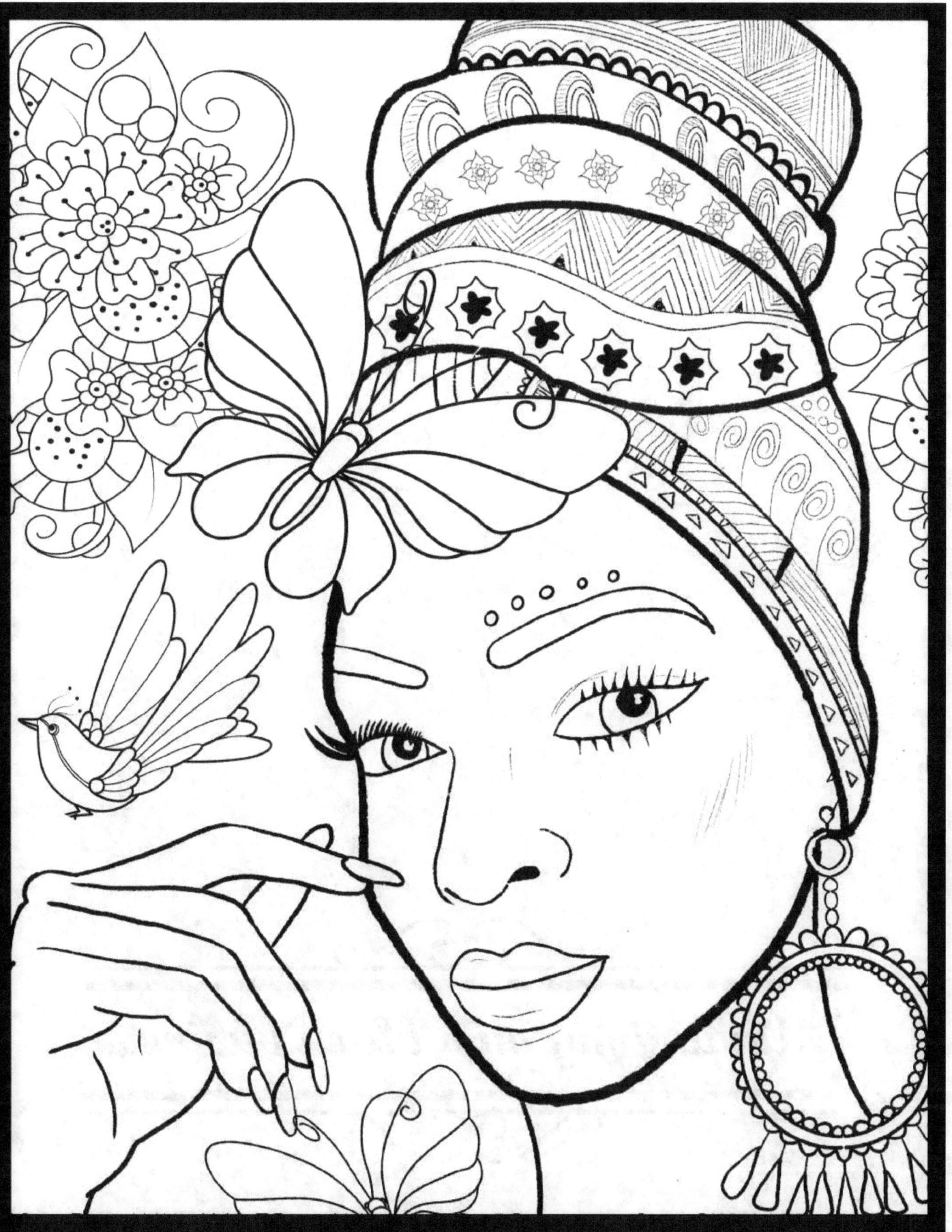

Minding my own black business

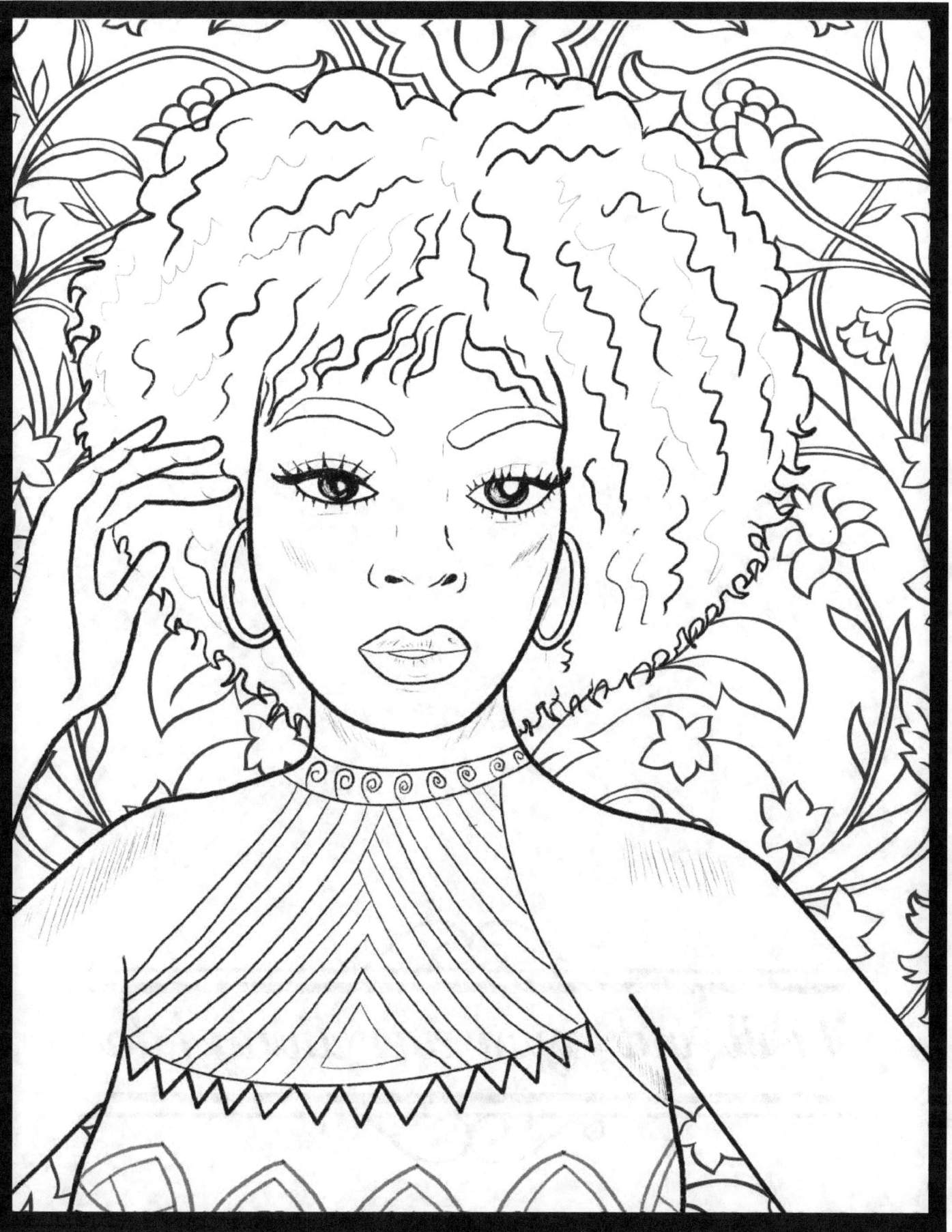

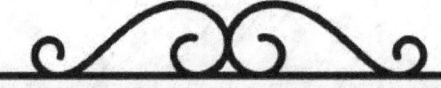

I will find joy in everything I do

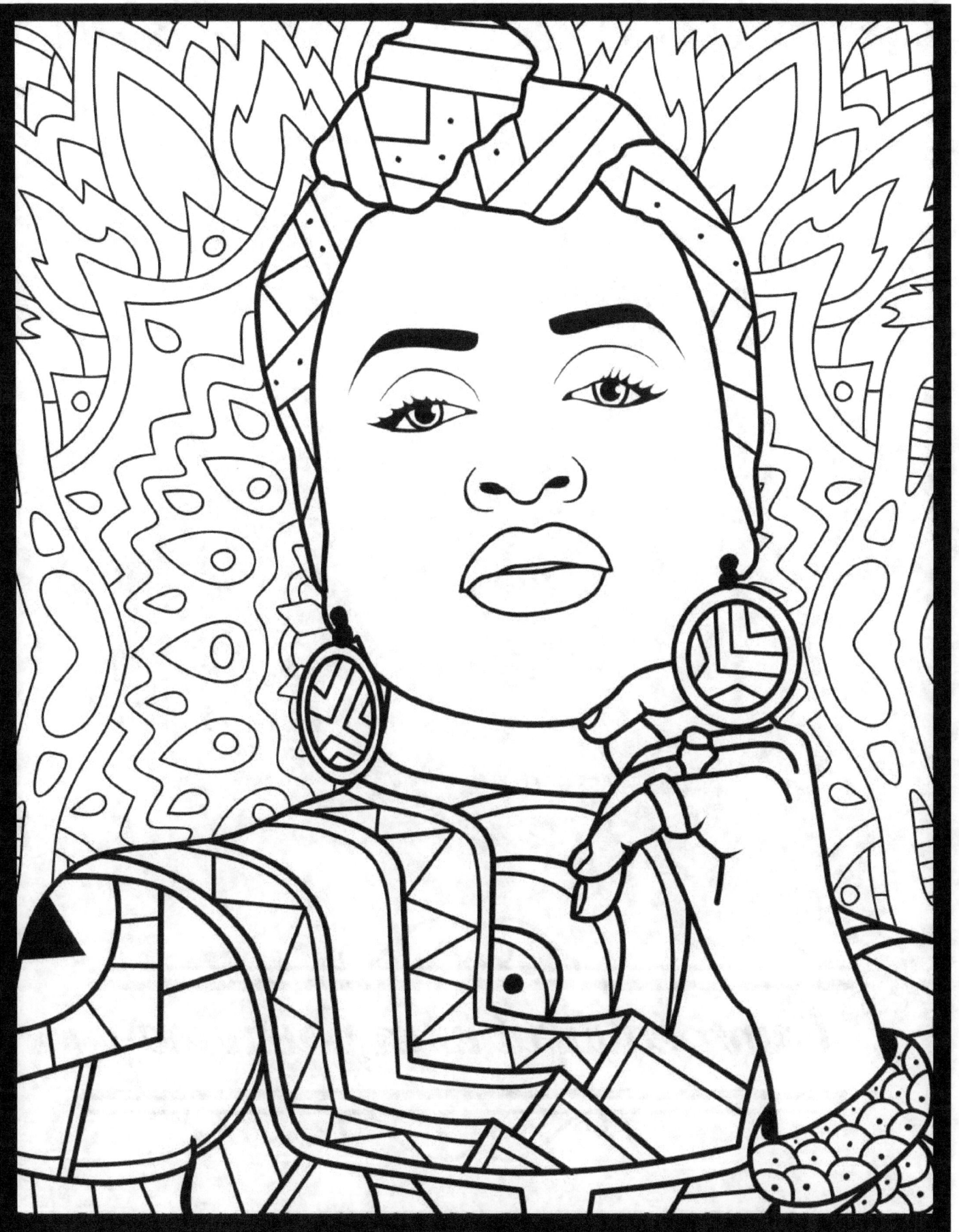

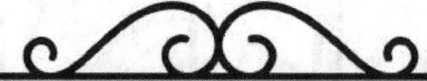

I am beautiful in my own way

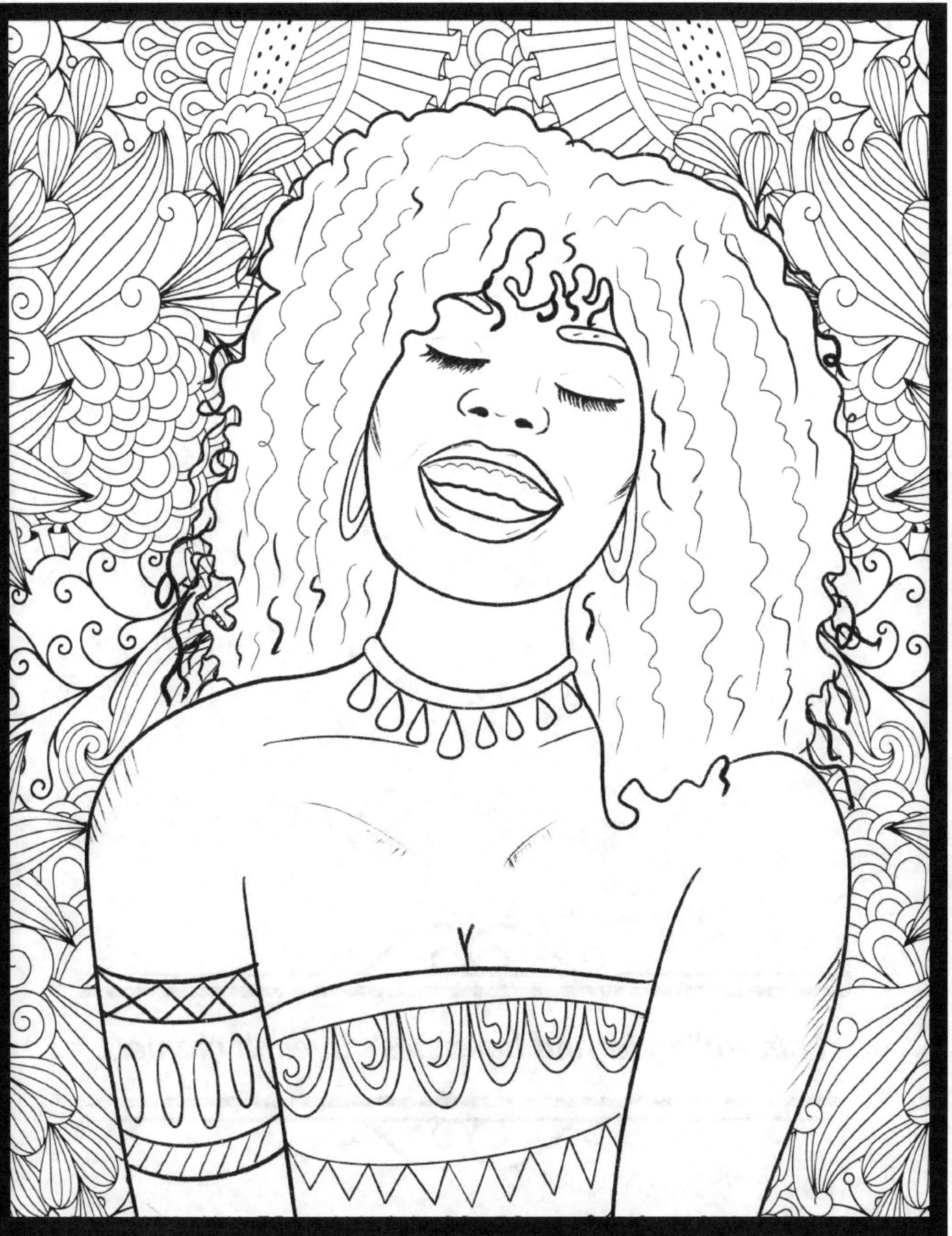

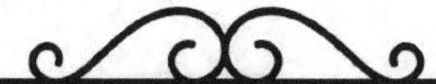

I am willing to find happiness in each moment

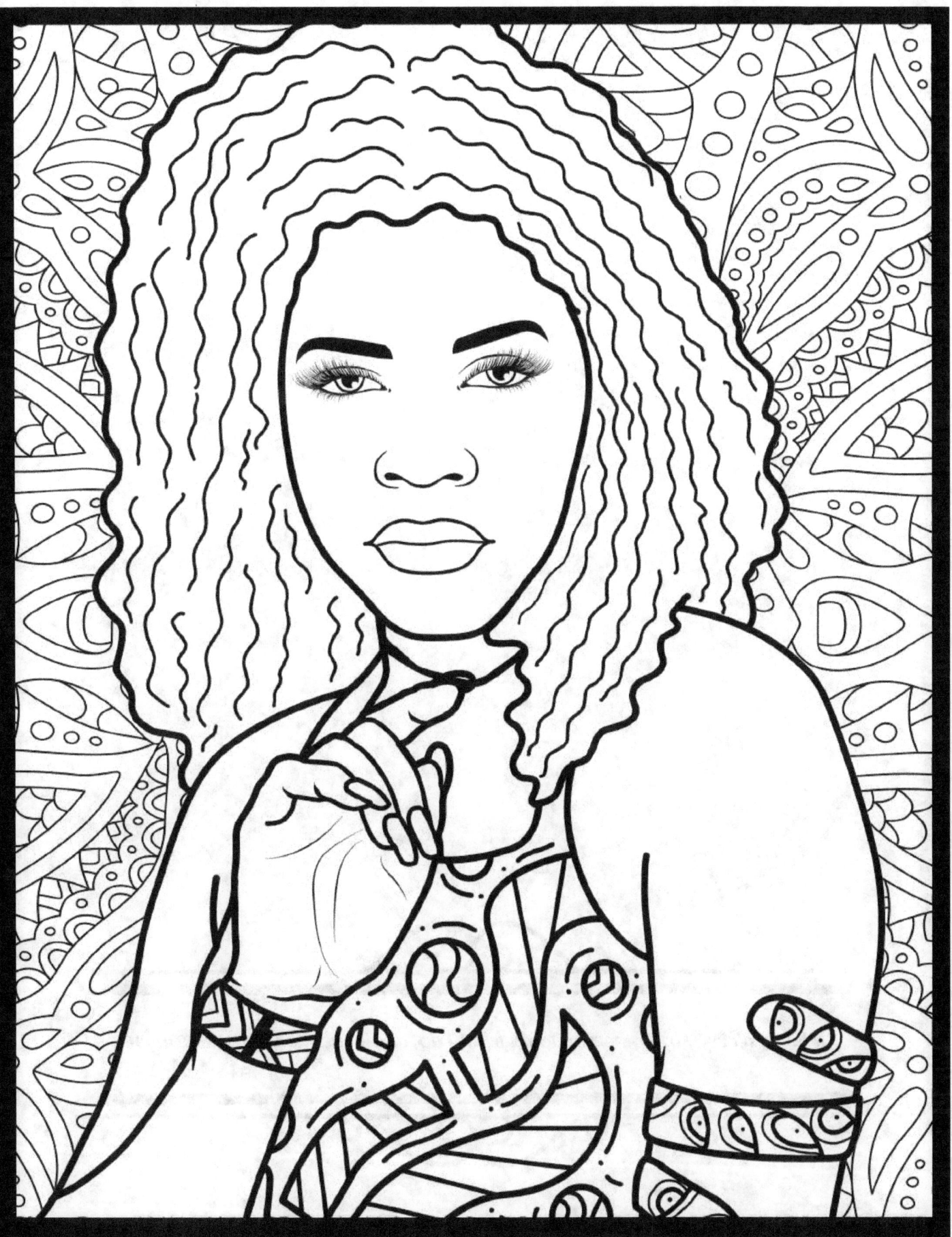

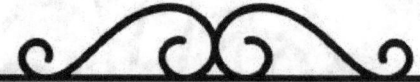

It takes a very strong person to do what I do, and I should be proud of myself

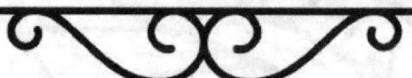

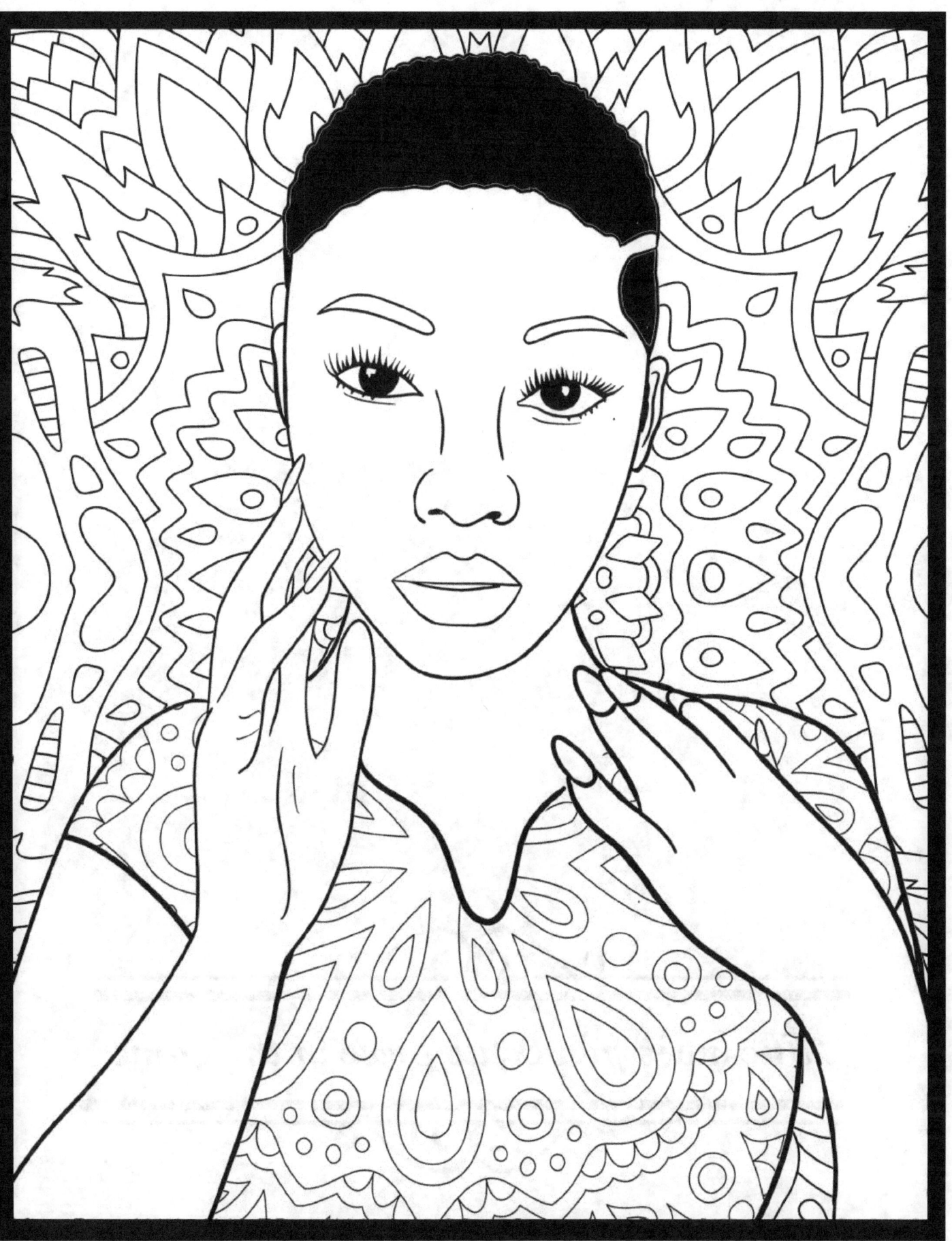

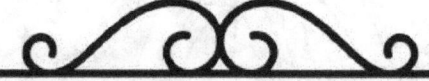

The most powerful piece in the game

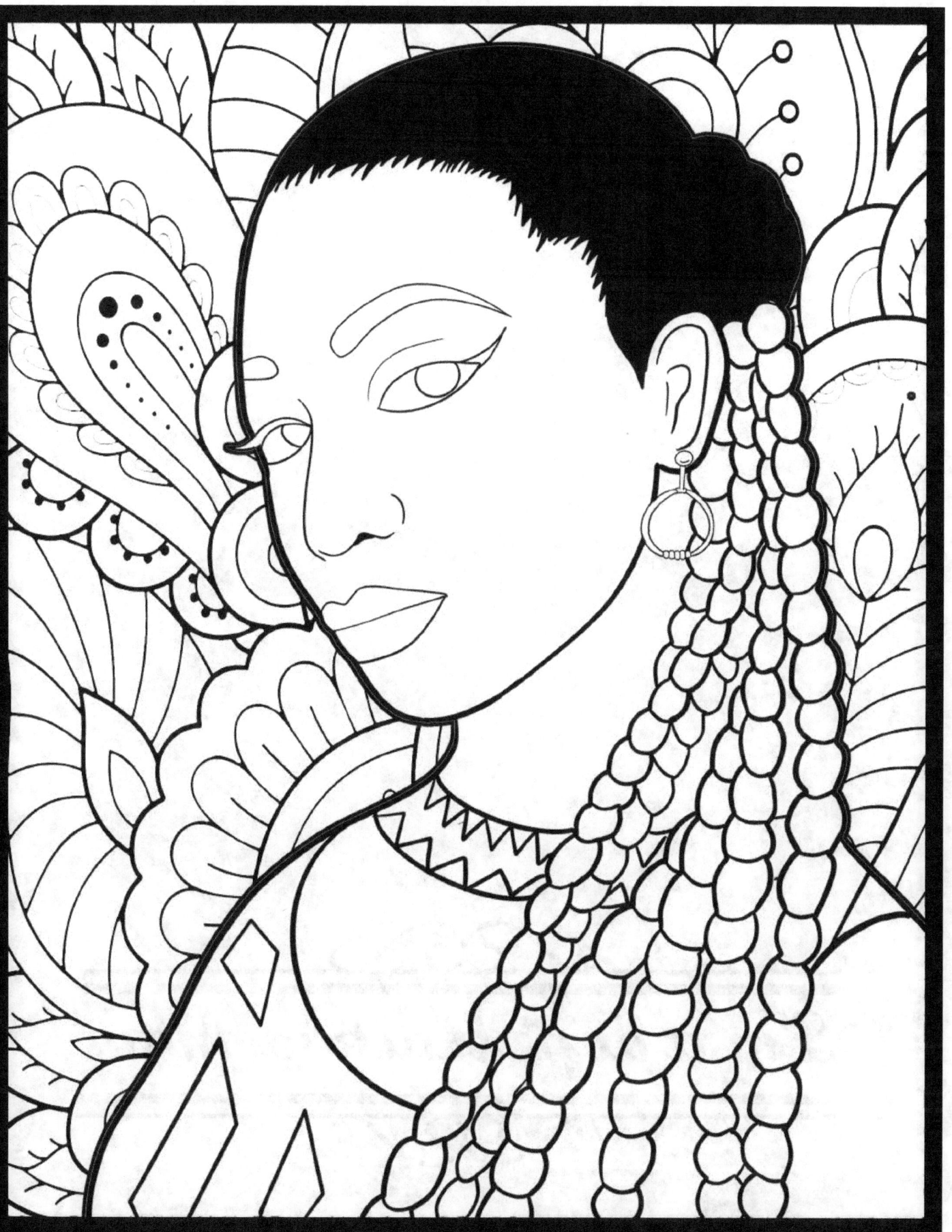

I'm a dope black woman

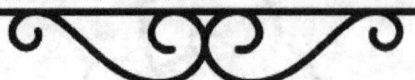